LET GO OF FEAR

LET GO OF FEAR

CARLOS G. VALLES

Triumph™ Books

New York, New York

Library of Congress Cataloging-in-Publication Data
Vālesa, Father, 1925–
    Let go of fear : tackling our worst emotion / by Carlos G. Valles.
       p.   cm.
    ISBN 0-8007-3004-6
    1. Fear.   I. Title.
    BF575.F2V34   1991
    152.4'6—dc20   90-46506
                                                                          CIP

Copyright © 1991 by Carlos G. Valles
Published by Triumph Books
An Imprint of Gleneida Publishing Group, Inc.
New York, New York
Printed in the United States of America
First Edition

A man's life is the story of his fears.

A. S. Neill

CONTENTS

Foreword
WINGS TO FLY

Once I saw it. On a lonely road in the warm Indian countryside between fields and crops and trees, far from any vestige of human habitation. I was pedaling gently on my bicycle—individual excursion on the freedom of two wheels without gasoline—feeling the hot air on my face, looking around as though in charge of the landscape, and letting my eyes rest on the green blessing that the yearly monsoon had brought on the tired earth. Not a person in sight. Only the birds and the squirrels and the bees. I moved on slowly, taking it all in. A leisurely ride on nature's own grounds. Only after a good while I noticed a subtle change. A strange stillness had invaded the scene. I sensed danger in the wind. I stopped the bicycle and watched intently.

Then suddenly I saw it. Something stood up in the low grass. A cobra, half-coiled, half-erect, with its hood spread out in majesty and its tongue flickering danger in the air. I followed its gaze, fixed on the branch of a bush slightly ahead and above. On the branch was a little bird paralyzed with fear. I had heard that snakes do that to birds. Now I was seeing it. The bird had wings, but could not fly. It had a voice, but could not sing. It was frozen, stiff, mesmerized. The snake knew its own power and had cast its spell. The prey would not escape, though it had the whole sky for its range. Fear held the bird. A jump from the grass, a sting from the deadly fang, and the lord of the air would fall under the earthbound enemy.

I stirred the breeze with my presence. The snake turned swiftly and looked angrily at me. I waved my arms and shouted human sounds. The cobra lowered itself reluctantly to the ground. There it stood still for a moment. Then it scurried away into the grass. A sense of relief swept through the landscape. The bush came alive again. The bird woke from its spell of death. It found its wings. And it flew.

That is what I want to do with this book. To stir the breeze. So that the bird may fly.

LET GO OF
FEAR

THE TRAUMA OF BIRTH

We never quite outlive it. We may take a lifetime to live down the shock of our first entry into this world. We carry down the imprint of our birth right to the moment of our death. We have no memory of it, and that makes us underrate the importance in our lives of the first event in them. But its influence is deeper precisely because we do not remember it. Events in our memory are under our control, since by remembering them we can understand them, accept them, integrate them; but events that escape our memory escape our direct control also, and can exert their influence, for good or evil, from the twilight shadows of permanent oblivion. Such is the case with our birth, a fundamental experience we all share and no one remembers. It marks us for life with the stamp of its suddenness, its surprise, its wild adventure into the realm of life. We can understand better the workings of our mind when we reflect on the circumstances of our birth.

The yet unborn child lives a secure and carefree existence in the friendly surroundings of its mother's womb. The gentle warmth, the restful darkness, the soft movements, the permanent caress of love, fill its tender senses. Nine months of undisturbed happiness to write a first chapter of hope in the biography of a new guest on earth. Forgotten period in our official records, but most eventful time in the shaping of our lives. Traits of our character were already fashioned there, together with our limbs and our features. A hidden factory of future personalities.

Once a young mother-to-be whom I had known since childhood came and asked me, with the blushing charm of her incipient maternity, how she could prepare herself to take the best possible care of her child right from the moment of its birth. I answered, with the same spontaneous intimacy she had had with me and her presence had inspired in me, that to wait for the moment of birth would be too late; the child was already with her, and the care had begun. "If you are relaxed, happy, and contented," I said, "the child inside you will notice it through the measure of your movements and the secret chemistry of your personal bond. It will sense from now that the world is friendly and life is beautiful, and something wonderful is waiting out there for it. On the contrary, if you are tense and nervous, if you are worried and upset and move in a hurry and talk with anger, the child within you will at once get the message, veiled but definite, that something is amiss, that there is danger outside and unfriendly surroundings in a world of fear. Your responsibility as a mother has already begun. Be easy in your mind and happy in your heart if you want your child to be born mentally healthy and to grow free from complexes." She understood, and I expressed my hope that the child had also somehow perceived through our conversation that someone else out there also cared for it and prayed for its welfare, and that it had a friend waiting to know its face and welcome its smile in the loving brotherhood that unites all people.

With greater or less fortune in the messages received and images prefigured, that first stage of a child upon earth soon reaches its end, and the child faces the momentous event of its bodily entrance into life as a separate individual. Nothing has prepared it for that unnerving experience of unexpected newness. Suddenly everything changes all around. Light shines on virgin pupils, strange voices enter untrained ears, while the unexposed tissues of folded lungs open up for the first time before the onrushing waves of life-giving air. The child hears for the first time its own voice, feels its own weight as its moist body hangs from the doctor's hands, receives on its open skin the first greetings of the atmosphere that will accompany its earthly career from now on in compulsory embrace. All that is new and strange and threatening. True, modern delivery rooms shade their lights and muffle their noises out of deference to the newborn, but eventually the encounter with the outside world is unavoidable, and the child faces the frontal attack of a hostile universe on his innocent senses. What is that noise and that glare, that heat and that cold, that movement and that hurry, which shake my body and even more my soul in this mad world of shrill voices and dazzling flashes into which I have been thrown? I was so comfortable before, so cozy, so secure, in the soft surroundings of my early home which I thought would be mine forever! Now I have to cry when I feel hungry, I have to crawl if I want to move. How can I survive, weak and alone, in this frightful struggle I am learning to call life?

The child has lost the primeval security of the womb, and the rest of its mortal existence will be a lifelong search for the lost safety. It has been deprived all of a sudden of all that guaranteed its daily life in its first human stage. Whatever the child needed by way of nourishment or protection was given to it before the child even had to ask. And now, without previous notice, the supply is cut and the contract is terminated. The child has to fend for itself, with the help, yes, of other people around, but also with the incipient fear that those people may fail it, may cut down gradually on their daily assistance, may eventually abandon the child to its own resources. The child has lost its security, and the fear of insecurity will haunt the child to the end of its days.

That basic fear will shape the child's needs, fashion its feelings, and direct its actions. The child will act in such a way as to ensure maximum security in all its growing needs. Security in food and shelter, in affection and relationship, and later on in employment and income, in social status and material welfare, and ultimately security after death in whatever the afterlife holds. The battle for security is on, and its vicissitudes are the chapters of a person's intimate biography.

The child searches for security, first of all, in its own mother, and clings to her in physical embrace, rewarding her attentions with the seducing tenderness of infant love. The child needs her closeness, her voice, her touch, to reassure itself that she is near and she cares and she will answer every call and supply every need. The loss of the original safety in the womb is somehow compensated by the fact that the child now becomes the center of the home and the focus of attention through day and night. The parents arrange their timetables accordingly, the mother is on leave from her work, and there is always someone nearby within wailing distance from the cradle. All is fine for a while, and the security seems to return to the infant's life.

But soon another crisis comes to threaten the growing baby. One day its mother takes it with her in the early morning, wrapped up in its finest trappings and accompanied by its favorite toys, stops at an unknown building, leaves the child in the hands of another woman with plentiful smiles on both sides, kisses the child with repeated insistence, turns back, and disappears rapidly down the stairs. The door closes, and the baby finds itself for the first time in the strange surroundings of a mother-less room. She is gone. Is that possible? Can she, who was the only one I trusted to stand by me always, abandon me like this? Can she leave me in the hands of another woman and disappear from my life? If I cannot trust her, how can I now trust this other woman, how can I trust anybody in my life? They just push me from one place to another, and I never know where I am going to land next. True, mother comes again and makes up for the lost hours with kisses and caresses, which only emphasize the separation and increase the suspicion. Is life something we ultimately have to live alone?

A greater trial awaits the small boy or girl if a smaller brother or sister is born into the family. Up until now I was the center of the family, and now I find myself suddenly displaced, and my throne given to a stranger and a rival who monopolizes my parents' attention day and night while I am left alone in a corner. A rival in my own home. How can I feel safe anymore when I am not safe in my own family? No explanations from the parents will allay the child's fears or make up for the lost safety. The child will eventually learn to accept the newcomer, and when both grow, they will be brothers and will love and support each other, and the original rivalry will be forgotten; but the insecurity that it created at the start has by then left its indelible mark on the hidden subconscious. The fear of being left alone, of being let down even by those who are closest and dearest, will be a haunting shadow along the paths of life. Nobody is ever safe.

Competition, once begun, spreads soon to the different fields of endeavor that await the young person with the increasing tension modern society imposes on its new candidates. Competition at school and college for results, first places, prizes, and scholarships. Competition for a job, salary, advancement, social status. Competition in games and in love. Hardly an area of human activity is left free from the daily friction of making one's way in conflict with others. One has to get ahead of others, and stay ahead in order to keep the advantages, once obtained. Thus we live under constant fear, felt with greater or lesser intensity but always present, of not obtaining what we desire or of losing it after we have obtained it. Ceaseless competition creates a state of insecurity, and insecurity breeds fear.

Commenting with a married friend on the fears of childhood, he told me his experience with his own son, no longer a child. The boy insisted on having his father by his side when going to sleep at night, and holding his hand till he fell asleep. The father would wait until the boy was asleep to withdraw his hand and free himself, but more often than not, the boy would notice the withdrawal even in his sleep and hold the hand tighter. Only much later and very, very gently could the father disentangle himself, while he always thought, he said, that one day the boy would have to go to sleep without a friendly hand to hold his own. Fears of the night that haunt even an innocent mind.

All fears are interconnected, and whatever their immediate object, all have in common the dark feeling of the threatening danger, all trace their origin back, in ominous genealogy, to the first loss of safety in the transit of birth, and all prefigure, with hidden but certain premonition, the last transit of death. The insecurity caused by the first birth is transferred on to the second birth into the next life. A person does not know for certain what awaits him when he leaves this world, as he did not know what awaited him when he came into it, and so the insecurity of death becomes the counterpart of the insecurity caused by birth, and one's life is thus bracketed between these two outstanding insecurities. He or she is born into a strange world, and leaves it for a stranger one—and always fears the unknown. The fear of death, fed by all subsidiary fears along a whole life, becomes the ultimate obstacle to be conquered by the valiant resolution of braving life and uncovering its terrors with faith and confidence. Fear of fear is the worst of fears. When we become ready to face our fears, we are on our way to overcoming them.

THE MAGIC CIRCLE

The Tagore household was a large one. Rabindranath was the fourteenth child of his parents, and his uncles and cousins lived under one roof in joint family. The result was that the supervision of the small children during most of the day was entrusted to servants. Rabindranath recalled later in life that when one servant got tired of playing with him, he would draw a circle on the floor of the room, with the child in the middle, and then say, "If you leave this circle, a monster will come and take you away." He reinforced his threat with the Ramayana story in which Lakshmana draws a line that Sita should not cross for her own protection, but she crosses it and is abducted by the demon Ravana. Then the servant would leave, and young Rabindranath was alone in the room, prisoner of the fatal boundary, and would not dare to cross it, spending in solitude the many hours the servant was away, a helpless heap of misery on the bare circle. Only after a long while, when the servant was good enough to come back and rub off the magic circumference, was the small child delivered again into life and freedom. And the memory of those lonely hours stayed with the wise man into his old age.

Frightful image of what fear does to someone. The black circle, the dire threat, the chilling fear, the bodily inability to cross the accursed line in a moral breakdown of mind and limb. A person, with the power of thought and imagination, of art and poetry and creation and joy, lies defeated on the cold floor of human despair. A thin line holds him in bondage, an irrational fear paralyzes his nerves. Such a person will not move, will not think, will not dare challenge the dark power that rules over his or her life in spiteful tyranny. It's so easy to draw the fateful line, and so impossible to cross it! The grown-ups will readily recognize the futility of the whimsical line that is a prison wall for the credulous children, but then will not recognize the lines and circles in their own lives that keep them from moving out into freedom and confidence. Subtle fears and hidden superstitions keep us from trying our utmost and giving of our best, from striking out boldly outside narrow boundaries and limited concepts into new adventures of thought and of life. Fear inhibits us and shrinks our lives.

The girls from the first class in a school were sitting for their first written test in their own school under the supervision of their own teacher. Halfway through the examination the teacher had to absent herself, and the principal of the school came to take her place. It was later observed that the girls had consistently written the first part of the paper better than the second, though all the questions were of the same difficulty. The presence of the feared principal instead of the familiar teacher had acted as an inhibiting factor on their tender minds.

And teachers and parents know of the universal complaint of students who claim they knew the answers perfectly well but were unable to recall them during the examination. While this can be an excuse for laziness or lack of brains, it can also be, and often in fact is, a real experience of an uncontrollable reflex in the presence of the threatening situation of an important examination. The mind goes blank, procedures are forgotten, the hand is stayed, and the

time passes mercilessly on an empty paper. When the final
bell rings and the hapless victim comes out, he will be able
to answer the questions correctly and solve the problems
adroitly, much to his own despair and that of those who
love him. He knew the answers but could not write them.

We have eyes and often cannot see, have minds and
often cannot think or draw the right conclusions or make
the right decisions, because fear comes on us, and our
natural faculties are impaired by the deadly presence of
the lifelong enemy.

Why are humans the only animals that do not swim
naturally? Because they are afraid of water. They are afraid
they will sink, and so at the first contact with the cold
surface, their bodies go stiff, their breathing stalls, their
hands and legs begin beating the water aimlessly, and they
will sink without mercy in the neutral waters that with a
minimum of cooperation would hold them cheerfully
afloat. There are schools to teach how to swim, crash
courses and individual tutors with guaranteed results in
record time. People have to be taught how to swim. And I
know how hard the teaching may become. I have failed to
convince a young boy he can float naturally in seawater if
only he lies still, arms outstretched, face to the sky, breathing rhythmically under the sun. He will try with my hand
holding his back as initial prop, but will bend up in fright
as soon as I withdraw my hand and his body knows it is
alone. He does not trust the water. He does not trust his
own body. He does not trust even his mind that tells him
a human body is slightly lighter than saltwater and floats on
it if left to itself. His mind thinks of danger, his mouth tastes
salt, his legs begin to sink, and he crumples up and strug-
gles to his feet to feel again the safety he longs for. The
moment he loses his fear, he will float.

As a young man, I was once riding a horse across a

river. I did not notice the moment the horse ceased treading on the riverbed and started swimming with me on top of it. It did it so naturally, so evenly, so matter-of-factly, that I knew we had swum only because I knew the river to be too deep to wade through. Again in younger days, I was in a group of boys when someone threw a hen into a pool of water for the fun of it. The hen did create quite a scene with obvious protests, but she swam unaided to safety amidst the cheers of the whole group. And dogs and mice and snakes and cows are expert swimmers. No school for them, no training, no crash courses. Nature itself teaches its creatures how to swim with the inward guidance of unfailing instinct. There is no reason to believe that a human being, as child of nature, does not possess that instinct. Surely we have it with us. But we stifle it, we push it down, we suppress it, with the blighting rationalization of our superior minds. We have imagination and forethought, and set them to work in caution and fear to protect us from fancied dangers. Our mind creates fears that hinder our progress. Instead of using our imagination to find new ways in the fields of thought and behavior, we use it to block the existing ones with invented fears. And we sink in the waters that were meant to be our path to new shores.

I knew a man who made a livelihood literally out of his lack of fear. He had no fear of heights, and his job was the maintenance of church domes, monument towers, high, inaccessible places on public buildings. Where anybody would have gone giddy and many a stomach would have churned with uneasiness, he stood, unruffled and cheerful, polishing slabs and clearing up crevices in dizzying heights. He could look up or down from his precarious perch without in the least feeling he could slip and fall with dire consequences. His lack of imagination was his protection and his means to earn a steady salary. There are, on the contrary, persons who cannot climb a height, stand on a ledge, or board a plane. The airlines keep their accident statistics low, but there are quite a few people who feel uneasy with the seat belt on, apart from the not so few who bluntly refuse to fly. Strange phobia of the jet era. People are known to have turned down a promotion or lost a job because of their unwillingness to fly. The job required frequent flying to distances where travel by road or rail would be impractical, and the positive advantage had to be given up because of the inner weakness. Something in their systems prevented them from taking a seat in a plane, and their careers suffered because of their bodily fears. Fear can take away a job, while lack of it can create one. If we add to the list the fear of meeting people, of blushing, of speaking in public, of open spaces, of closed spaces, and many more kinds which we may not even have thought of but which are painfully real to more people than we care to imagine, we shall have a picture of the daily distress and downright suffering that fear in its many aspects inflicts on humankind.

There are varied therapies to deal with concrete phobias, and many people find relief in expert treatment. A book like this one is no substitute for professional help, but it can create the climate, the inner atmosphere, that alerts the mind and directs the senses to uncover hidden fears and tackle them with confidence and skill. For a start, the simple realization that fear occupies a much larger space in our life than we are usually willing to admit is an essential condition for healing. Recently, in a long talk with a friendly person, I spoke of the many fears I had discovered in myself, their negative effects on me, and the way I had gotten rid of some of them. I admit that my aim in talking of myself was to make him think about himself, as I had surmised that he too could benefit from a recognition and analysis of his own fears. My discomfiture was considerable when he spoke condescendingly and said, "I understand how the circumstances of your life have led you to experience all those fears, and I surely appreciate what you are doing about them. For my part, my life from childhood has always been a very healthy one. I have never experienced any serious fear and I am free and at ease in that matter. It was nice to listen to you." I hope this book is a little more productive than that conversation was.

A SNAKE IN MY DREAMS

We are aware of some of our fears. Bodily fears or mental fears. We may be afraid of darkness, of contagious diseases, of the sight of blood, of death. And we know it. We can list our fears, even tick off the relevant items in lists provided for this purpose in psychological manuals. We can admit to ourselves and even to others that we are afraid of certain things and we feel anxious in certain circumstances. It is, however, important to realize that some of our fears are unconscious too, and we are not aware of them. These are the ones that do us the most harm.

When we know we have a certain fear, we can face it, can tackle it, can try ways and means to minimize it and even make it disappear altogether from our life or at least learn to live with it. When we are unaware of our own fears, when we deny them, refuse to see them, ignore them, they are free to exert their baneful influence undisturbed, and we are the losers. To be afraid is supposed to be something disgraceful, and that may be why we try to cover up our fears not only before others but all the more before ourselves, since it is in our eyes that we want to preserve our own image as courageous, fearless, and unafraid. We do not want to lose face before ourselves, and so we put up a bold front, draw up our chin, and proclaim ourselves to be unaffected by common fears or apprehensions. Meanwhile the fear has gone underground and, in the dark, plots effective attacks on our defenseless citadel. It is to our own advantage to give ourselves the freedom to look at our own fears without shame or misgivings, rather than pretend we are not afraid of anything. We *are* afraid, and we should be the first to know it and to own up to it.

Once, while traveling abroad, I had a dream at night that I had lost my passport and was stranded in a foreign airport without help and with no resolution to my problem. It was a most disturbing nightmare, so much so that I woke up from sheer distress to find out, with immense relief, that it had only been a bad dream. The curious fact is that consciously I had not been aware that I was afraid of losing my passport. I am an experienced traveler, I take good care of my belongings, and in the worst case I know how to handle a crisis and make up for a lost passport. I am not going to be disturbed by a remote possibility that is only the wild speculation of a weak mind. If I were to worry about such contingencies, I would never leave my house. No, I am not afraid of losing my passport. And yet I was.

My subconscious knew it and brought up in the shadows of the night what I was refusing in the light of day. I was afraid, I was uneasy, I was insecure, and I was pushing down all those disreputable feelings into the dark recesses of my mind, to show to myself and to the world that I was brave and unafraid, while all along I was deeply afraid that I might land in serious difficulty. Curiously, the nightmare recurred again after a few nights. It must have been quite a deep-rooted fear, and yet I was blissfully unaware of it. How many more fears, big and small, must be prowling the dark galleries of my unconscious, a standing danger to my peace and happiness, under the security they draw from my refusal to acknowledge them!

Recently, in another dream, I vividly saw a cobra close to my feet and ready to strike, and the effect was so real that, fully asleep, I struck out in self-defense and violently hit the menacing hood with my foot. What I hit, in fact, was the wall against which my beds rests, and the wild stroke brought such a sharp pain to my brave foot that I woke up in agony, not quite knowing yet whether I had hit the cobra or the cobra had hit me. For days after, I had to limp on a bandaged big toe, while fighting the embarrassment of answering well-meant inquiries about my injured foot. Friends smiled wistfully when I told them I had kicked the wall in a dream. Was everything well with me? Not quite. The worst was that I have always accepted the Gestalt way of dealing with dreams, according to which the objects of our dreams are projections of our own selves, disowned during the day and resurrected in the night under the freedom of uncensored display. In other words, the cobra was myself, some aspect in me, some tendency or some belief or some practice in me of which I was secretly afraid while it kept fighting back with poison in its fangs. And, again, all that play of fears and defenses was going on in me without my taking any notice of it. During the day the fearless mask, and at night the venomous snake. Scope and challenge for greater self-knowledge. It was not only my big toe that needed a bandage, but some parts of my mind too.

Apart from hiding itself from our view, fear knows also how to disguise itself under the cloak of other more respectable emotions, so that it can exert its influence without revealing its presence. A favorite disguise for fear is anger or sadness. A person cannot be afraid and angry at the same time, and so he may often bring the cover of anger to hide the reality of fear. A psychologist tells of an experience he had as a youth. His parents had moved to another town, and he transferred in midterm to another school. There, he was subjected to ragging, which resulted in a fight with the school bully. He made the mistake of knocking down his adversary, and immediately a dozen boys were on him and pinned him to the ground under the weight of their bodies. He was mortally afraid under the impossible burden when suddenly he uttered a wild cry, lifted himself against the human wall, and let go at all around him with hands and feet in a frenzy of savage strength. In him, anger had replaced fear. His adversaries retreated in a circle, and the appearance of a teacher ended the fight. In his fear, he was intimidated and lost his strength, but when anger took over, his fear was forgotten and strength returned in full measure. When the anger subsided, the fear came up again and made him wonder what would happen next. Fortunately his schoolmates had been frightened by his display of muscle, and it was now their turn to be afraid. Their ragging ended.

If anger covers up for fear, sadness can cover up for anger and therefore ultimately for fear too. An acute fear cannot last long, and a way for it to continue is to dissolve itself into sadness that has the similar effect of paralyzing the soul under the hazy burden of undefined adversity. It is easier to say "I feel sad" than to say "I am afraid," and so sadness takes the place of fear and lengthens its damaging reign over us. Even the best of us experience long spells of blurred sadness in which the burden of despondency is increased by the apparent lack of reason for it. Why do I feel this way? Why am I sad without a reason I can pinpoint to account for this extended moodiness? When will this end? Where will it leave me? The bonds of sadness can tie heart and limb with freezing efficiency. We languish under sadness as we shivered

under fear. Our negative feelings are ultimately the many
faces of fear.

Hatred also can be distorted fear. We hate what we fear.
A way of protecting ourselves from a menacing situation is
to hate whatever is involved in it, particularly the persons
who cause it. By hating those persons, we remove them
from our life, we put a safe distance between them and us,
we eliminate their influence on us, so we no longer fear
those we have emotionally cut off from us by hating them.
If hatred seems an extreme word, we might as well apply
the principle to lesser dislikes or disinclinations. A persistent dislike of a person may have its origin in a hidden fear
of what that person may do to us. Then, even when the
circumstances of fear may disappear, the dislike irrationally continues and a relationship is blocked. Behind the
open or veiled declaration "I hate him," we can hear the
echo of the original feeling, "I fear him."

Jealousy in love is only fear of not being loved, fear that
we may lose the person we love or need, because of his or
her attraction to another person, and so we hate this other
person and mentally wish his or her destruction to ensure
our safety. Affective insecurity is the breeding ground for
jealousy, and insecurity is the mild beginning of fear.

A little analysis will show, without distorting perspectives, that all our negative feelings can ultimately be traced
to fear. In broad but true simplification we can say that
there are only two basic human emotions, one positive
and the other negative. The positive one is love, and the
negative fear. One more way to realize the importance of
fear in our lives.

A LITTLE SHIELD

Though fear is the basic negative emotion in our system, still there are some positive aspects to it, and it is only fair to recognize them. This will also make it easier for us to accept our fears and look them in the face. If they can be put to some good use, we may reconcile ourselves after all to the fact that we have fears, and we may identify them more easily. All that will be to our advantage.

The first positive role of fear is to protect us. When a danger appears, and the danger may well be real, fear of it leads us to seek protection and thus ensure safety. Some animals literally live on fear. Outstanding among them are the squirrels that play at my window and almost share my room with me in imposed partnership. They nibble on my curtain, pilfer my socks at night, race each other across my bed, and look disdainfully at me while I work at my typewriter, resigned to my fate. They are familiar with me, and they should know by now from our long acquaintance that no harm will come to them from me. And yet they fear me. The slightest motion of my hand, even a gentle movement of my body, sends them scurrying out of the window and across space onto the tree outside, and in it, to its outer side, from which they point at me their funny triangular faces and wait for perfect stillness to resume their endless chase through all available space. Fear is their defense. They have no strength, no weapon, no muscle or claws. But they have fear, and that saves them. They fly before the shadow of danger. And their safety is in their flight. They sense the smallest sign of possible trouble and they react to it with utmost swiftness by turning tail and making themselves scarce. Their bushy tails up in the wind seem to be the aerials that monitor danger signals and transmit them with swift efficiency to brain and legs for immediate action. One jump and they are out of sight. Impossible to lay hands on them. Their reflexes are quicker than man's because they depend on them for their life. They are born with the innate sense of fear to shield them in an unfriendly world.

Once, a friend of mine took a recently born baby squirrel in his hand to pet it and feed it, but before he could do that, the little animal died in his hand . . . of fright. The contact of a human hand had been too much for an organism built on fear, and it had shivered to death in the foreign embrace. Tragedy of an overdrawn instinct. And a lesson to us to enjoy the protection of our fears without letting them stifle our life.

To see deer in their own habitat, one has to go to Africa. Herds of all kinds and all names and all sizes on the aboriginal plains. With them, the fear instinct is in the group. They all graze together in the tall grass; they all move together, seemingly unconcerned, among birds and breezes and noises. But there are noises and noises, and the deer know the difference. As soon as the wrong note strikes the air, all heads move simultaneously and all ears turn in the same direction. The secret signal comes, and all bounce as one body, a hundred graceful parallel arcs of gold on the green carpet, and all disappear together on the same horizon. All obey a communal fear in practiced unison. Fear and speed are the protection of the species. If they are to survive in the jungle, they need their sensitive radar and their springlike legs. The moment they lower their defenses, they will fall prey to the lord of the jungle. A fearless antelope will not live long in the African plains.

Our ancestors too lived in the jungle and needed fear for their survival. This is the fear that has since then been programmed into the human organism and that we inherit with our bodies and our minds. Fear as a withdrawal reflex when circumstances seem adverse for life. Also the fear that is transformed into sadness and dejection, and which overcame primitive peoples when the going was rough, when the weather was cold and game was scarce in the wilderness. To save energy, to live through a severe winter, to nurse a wound or to survive a fever, our ancestors slumped into protective hibernation to withdraw into minimal consumption for a period of time before they resumed normal activity in fullness of health. That same reflex operates in us when we face adverse circumstances, when we pass through a crisis, when we need to save energy in the winters of life and we find ourselves in low spirits and depressed mood. That is nature working in us for survival. Our organism lies low that it may come to full strength again. We dislike those periods of dark weather and somber thoughts, but they too have a purpose in the totality of our existence. We cannot always be at a peak, and we need the valleys in our lives to complete the complex itinerary of our journey through earth.

Another positive aspect of fear is paradoxically opposite to its other effects, but is no less true. I have mentioned that fear can paralyze a student in an examination, but it can also work him up to do better in it. Some artists declare that unless they work themselves up to a certain degree of anxiety, they cannot give of their best on the stage. A certain amount of tension can help performance, and many of us work better under pressure. When we have all the time in the world and all the facilities available, we are prone to relax and procrastinate and do a poor job, whereas if we have to turn in an important result in record time, we declare an emergency, draw on all our faculties, strain every resource, and come up with a splendid performance. A little bit of adrenaline speeds up our processes and enlivens our reactions. In all these cases it is a mild dose of fear that works positively; an excessive amount of it will normally have the opposite effect I mentioned before, namely the freezing of faculties and shutting off of the power to react in full capacity. A chess master once revealed that the best thing that could happen to him in a tournament was to lose his first game. Then he was sure to strain every nerve, summon all his resources, and make sure of the eventual victory. If he began by an easy win, he was likely to grow overconfident, let games drift, and come out a loser.

A bit of competition, even with the anxiety and strain it generates, can help to bring out the best in us. The danger comes when competition increases and rules every department of life with its burden of worry and stress. The optimum situation would be the faculty to engage the fullness of our strength without any appeal to anxiety or fear, but out of the peaceful resolution always to do the best we can do irrespective of appreciation or results. This is a rare achievement.

Shyness is a lesser manifestation of fear, yet it too keeps us from full action and inhibits best results. Cheeks burn, eyes drop, tongue gets tied up, and nothing is said and nothing is done when something is expected of the bashful person. Shyness earns no bread, goes the proverb. A shy person will not get his due in this competitive world where one has to fight not just to win new rights but to protect old ones. Protecting one's place in a line, getting attention in a shop with many customers, applying and striving to obtain a job, are circumstances that can be trying enough for an even-tempered person; but they can become sheer agony for the shy applicant. A certain amount of boldness is necessary to make one's way in life and keep one's rightful place in society.

I know the sufferings of a shy young man who for a time could find only the job of selling Bibles from door to door. Every knock at a door was a racking pain, every smile a conquest, every sale an untold relief. God must have appreciated the efforts of the young man, who was not even a Christian. At the other extreme is the aggressive sales agent, and we all would benefit if he would bring a little shyness into his manners even if his sales dropped.

Shyness, for all the handicap it brings, has its own charm and, just as fear, can also protect us from danger. Mahatma Gandhi in his autobiography tells with naive innocence the story of how his virtue was put to the test in a rather crude way. Before sailing for England, he had taken a vow not to touch women, wine, or meat, as only on that condition would his mother allow him to go. When the ship stopped in a harbor on the way, Gandhi went ashore with a fellow traveler, and this man soon brought two women, went himself with one, and left the other with Gandhi in a private room. Gandhi was no fool and knew well the intention. But he was shy, and he sat down motionless while the girl did the same by his side. After a while he just got up and opened the door. The girl understood and left. Gandhi gave this title to that chapter in his autobiography: "Shyness: My Shield." It is only fair to remark, though, that he grew to overcome his shyness in the service of his country, and met viceroys and addressed crowds and led movements in his fight for freedom. But he was always grateful for the little shield that had protected him in an awkward moment. The man who brought freedom to India was a shy man.

THE SACRIFICE OF THE HORSE

Fear plays another important role in the shaping of our mind if we know how to interpret it and put it to good use. Briefly it is this. Fear marks the boundaries of our personality, and thereby shows us the direction along which we can expand that personality, should we so desire. The idea is simple and its consequences far-reaching. It is well worth reflecting about.

That we have boundaries in our life is a matter of experience. There are situations, places, persons, with whom we feel perfectly at ease, and we can take in all that comes from them, respond, and interact with utmost confidence. Those are the circumstances of our daily life with which we are familiar and feel at home. As more unfamiliar situations come up, however, we instinctively become self-conscious and our defenses go up. In the presence of strange persons or threatening events we become wary, suspicious, and afraid. The closer we approach the limits of familiarity, the greater trepidation we feel and the more precautions we take. And if we really get close to the boundary, we experience real fright and long to retreat as soon as possible into the safety of our daily surroundings. The frontiers of fear mark the territory in which we feel at ease and operate normally.

Animals, too, have their territories. In the jungle or on the fields, in the streets of the city or even in the open skies, groups or pairs of animals mark their definite boundaries with cartographic accuracy and stick to them in all their wandering and their hunting while they zealously fend off intruders and fight for privacy. To us humans, those animal boundaries may be invisible, but animals recognize them and know well the danger involved in trespassing them. Some species mark them bodily, as rabbits with their droppings or rhinoceroses with their urine. In turn, the lion marks them with the majesty of its presence and the reach of its roar. But the boundary is there, publicly announced and universally respected.

There is a pair of lizards that, together with the squirrels I mentioned, share my room with me in happy coexistence. As our needs differ, and so does our food, none of us is a threat or a rival to any other. So long as that pair of lizards is with me, no other lizard will enter my room, and any that dare to wave their tails near my window will be immediately chased away by my tenants with angry efficiency. But then I have observed that when the incumbents disappear through death or departure, my room is immediately occupied by a new pair. There seems to be a well-run agency that informs wait-listed lizards of vacant apartments and allots them to the best applicant. My room is never without its pair of lizards, and never with more. Territories seem to be clearly marked and reverently accepted. And I am sure they consider themselves the owners of the room, and me only a tenant.

I had another boundary adventure with animals, this time with a little unpleasantness. I was once walking meditatively on the terrace of our building when suddenly my head was hit from behind by the sharp talons of a swooping kite. It drew blood before I drove it back into the sky with irate protest. It left me badly bruised and confused. What had happened? I soon found out. The kite was new to our neighborhood and had built its nest on a tree just touching our terrace, and this was the time for it to hatch its brood. It was consequently suspicious of any approaching figure, and my presence on the adjoining terrace was a threat to its family. Again a question of territory. I, unaware of the ways the sky is marked by its inhabitants, had trespassed on another's boundary, and had paid for it. And I had no known way of signaling to the kite that part of the terrace at least was mine. I did not learn its language of shrill shrieks. But I did learn to watch the back of my head when walking on the terrace thereafter.

We humans have our territories too, more subtle but as clear and definite as the parcels of land and the portions of sky. Our territory is not only land and persons but, more characteristically, ideas and principles and models of behavior. We feel comfortable within a certain range of concepts and values, of ways of understanding life and shaping our conduct. We can talk freely with people whose assumptions are fairly the same as ours, and think consistently along the lines we have always thought, with a little variation for entertainment, but without any fundamental change. If we encounter new ideas, bold concepts, daring views on life and society and religion and morals, we instinctively draw ourselves up, grow stiff, and take notice. Danger ahead. Unfamiliar ground. Be careful. Switch off. Turn back. Safety first. And we withdraw into our mental territory to enjoy in undisturbed peace the standard ideas in the standard way.

Here comes the point. The red signal of danger came up when we approached the end of our mental map. If we want to remain forever on familiar ground, all we have to do is turn back and return to base. On the other hand, if we feel inclined to explore new lands in the thrilling adventures of the mind, that red signal can be a useful pointer for us. Fear has signaled the end of our private land . . . and therefore the beginning of uncharted continents for us to explore. Fear marks for us directions of growth. If we want to grow in spirit, in courage, in faith, and in understanding, we can consult our fears and observe where they point. Then follow their lead in confidence. The rule is almost "If you are afraid of it . . . do it!" With common sense always, of course, and a balanced sense of responsibility, but with a cheerful mind and a brave spirit.

Our fears have shown us our weak points, our deficiencies, our shortcomings, and so to improve our character, brighten the future, and enlarge our boundaries, we thank our fears for their valuable information and set about working on it by exploring the very lands they are closing before us. It's as simple as that. That is why our fears are so important for our development. The frontiers of fear are the frontiers of growth. To break new frontiers, we can now consult our fears and study the landscapes they are hiding from our view. Maybe we shall then feel like venturing into new lands until new frontiers stop us . . . and we wait to gather again the strength to go beyond them in the unending discovery that is life.

In India we still celebrate each year an ancient festival called "The Breaking of Frontiers" (in Sanskrit, *simollanghan*). It is the festival of *Dassera*, or "tenth day," after *Navratri*, that is, the "nine nights" that all our girls spend in endless dances round and round the image of Mother Earth with a joy and a vitality that not only represent but make real before us the place of woman as the fountainhead of creation and the source of all life on fertile earth. I have never seen anything like the speed, color, rhythm, and endurance of those girls in the sacred artistic rite, night after night, under the tireless blessing of youthful beauty. (How can I punish a girl who sleeps next day through my mathematics class when I know she was dancing last night and will need all her energy to dance again tonight in the ancient liturgy of song and dance?) When the dances are over and nature has been worshiped, we are ready to remember and consider the ancient rite that gave name to the festival and meaning to its message. This part of the rite is not enacted anymore, but its memory remains from the days when there were kings in the lands of India, and each one fought to enlarge the limits of his kingdom, and soldiers rode on horses to fight the frontier battles. I describe the rite as it took place in olden days, and then explain its permanent meaning beyond horses and battles and kings.

The festival took place in the fall, and that strategic situation in the course of the seasons gave it its character and marked its importance. The rainy season was over, the crop had been harvested, and the cold of winter had not yet set in. Work in the fields had come to an end, the men were back home, and the king of the land would now take advantage of their enforced idleness and draft them into his army for the months in which there was no work in the fields till the next sowing. Thus the army was ready, and so was the king to lead it. The king wanted to enlarge his domains and conquer new lands for prosperity and power. How would he choose the lands for invasion, the direction for his army to advance? Here comes the interesting point. He would not choose for himself, but would let the gods decide for him through the mute cooperation of a symbol of conquest: a horse.

The best horse from the royal stables had been chosen, and it was now brought in front of the people and let free to roam at will. Wherever it went, the army went behind it, and whatever land it trampled upon would be annexed to the kingdom. If another army came to defend that land, the horse's army would fight to defend its sacred symbol and win the right over the land. Thus would the horse continue his sovereign wanderings at pleasure through the whole fighting year, while the army won battles and the king enlarged his kingdom. The next rains signaled the end of the campaign, the army returned, the men went back to their work in the fields, the new frontiers were consolidated, and the unknowing hero of the political expansion, the royal horse, was fed and honored by the whole people. The honor, however, did not last long. At the end of the year, before a new horse would be chosen for the new campaign, the previous horse was worshiped for the last time, and then sacrificed to return to the gods in the awkward gesture of love unto destruction, their own gift to man. The whole rite was consequently called the *ashwamedha*, or "sacrifice of the horse."

Today, of course, there is no horse and no sacrifice, and no battles among kings and no change of frontiers, when the land is one and the kings have lost their crowns; and I wonder as I read the ancient books and take part in the modern festival how many know today the meaning of these days and the challenge of these rites. And I read into them now a meaning that goes beyond the material conquest of acres of land into the more intimate battles of the spirit, the breaking of boundaries of mind and custom, and the thrust into new ideals and dreams and realities to make true in our lives what lies beyond us now but can be part of our land, that is, our mind and our life, if we follow the best of our instincts, strike out in courage, and make our own new ways of thinking and new patterns of behavior. Let the horse free, let imagination wander at will, let creativity surge in us untrammeled and unhindered into any direction and through any field and in any form to give us new perspectives and new kingdoms as we conquer them with the boldness of our courage and the strength of our faith.

This is the conquest of fear, the widening of boundaries, the opening up of new spaces in which to think and to live. And the basis of the festival in our souls is the knowledge of our own fears, the consciousness of our weaknesses, the awareness of our limitations. It is knowledge that liberates us and shows the path to progress. The breaking of frontiers is the festival of growth.

THE FEAR OF SUCCESS

The frontiers of fear are directions for growth. We should know that the fundamental fear that blocks our horizons and defeats our progress is the fear of success. The paradoxical, irrational, and yet universal fear of success. Thus our fears point literally to our successes, and the exploration into the forbidden land takes us nearer our goals.

Why should we be afraid of success? Most people are unaware of such a fright and will even deny it if it is mentioned to them. Afraid of success? Why should we be? In fact, it is of failure that we are afraid, not of success. We desire and strive for success with all our might as a social, psychological, and financial need. Nobody is afraid of passing an examination; what many are afraid of is failing in it. Nobody is afraid of getting a job, while all are afraid of losing the one they have. Success is always welcome, and it is only failure that is feared. This is a universal experience.

Yes, on the surface. Deep down, things are different. A student does not appear for an examination, an applicant turns down a job, a writer holds back a manuscript ready for publication, a painter never finishes a masterpiece. Fear? Yes. Of what? Not necessarily of failing in the examination or of displeasing the critics with the book or the painting, but often of exactly the opposite, that is, of obtaining the degree or achieving fame. There may be a block that bars the way to success for the unconscious mind. The student may feel he does not deserve success, and the artist may fear that sudden recognition will throw an impossible burden on him. Why did Brahms keep his first symphony unpublished for twenty years? Why did George Cantor wait as long to make known his theory of transfinite numbers? They feared fame, they drew back from the moment of glory, they postponed the inevitable triumph that would impose heavy demands on them. In fact, though Brahms did write three more symphonies after his first one, Cantor did not make any other substantial contribution to mathematical knowledge besides his transfinite numbers, which he discovered in his youth and published in ripe middle age. Fear of success kept them from publishing their successes.

A young man may often feel that he does not deserve success. The hidden commandment that he should not be more successful than his parents, the secret self-punishment for having hated his parents or his brothers and sisters, and, more viciously but not impossibly, the unconscious vengeance on his parents for imagined wrongs and imposed behavior, depriving them of the fruit of their hopes by becoming a failure himself. Twisted machinations of unconfessed guilt, but not altogether unreal or unlikely.

Here is a girl who could command success in any sphere of life, yet when I meet her I notice she is shabbily dressed, has grown fat, and informs me she is not completing her studies. What had happened? Some unconvincing explanations on the surface, and the real reason deeper down. She had been jealous of her younger sister ever since the newcomer at birth ousted her from her privileged place in the home, and that mean attitude had bred guilt in later years. Now she could not allow herself to succeed beyond her younger sister's success, and though she had better brains and better looks, she would not study further or try for a better match. Her guilty conscience would not allow her to be successful. To be successful would be the ultimate treason in the family circle, and so she could not afford it. She had come to fear success and to fight it effectively.

Such are the strange but real workings of the human mind. In this case its very outlandishness made plain its meaning, but without reaching so far, we too may find ourselves in similar though lesser straits, not quite as recognizable but no less dangerous to our welfare and advancement. A sense of unworthiness may keep us from trying hard and forging ahead, and may even make us draw back when we approach success, and defeat it. Even a certain way of proposing virtue as the way of sufferings and humiliations can have the negative side effect of making us feel guilty if we achieve success, and consequently we fear it. If divine strength works through human weakness, how can I court success and seek triumph? A contradiction is set up within us between the obvious urge to work and strive and bear fruit on the one hand, and the scruple to accept victory on the other. This absurd but real tension can cause great harm.

The threat of success comes from the obligations it imposes on the successful person. If a student comes out first in an examination, the student's parents, relatives, and friends will expect him or her to keep up the grade in the next examination and so on till the end of the student's academic career. The student has done it once, thereby proving that it can be done. Then why not again? The student has the brains, or else would not have scored so high that time. There is no reason not to repeat the performance, unless it is laziness or negligence. Once an achiever, always an achiever. The subconscious knows that, and that is why it may choose to avoid the awesome responsibility by shirking the issue. Fail, and escape.

Every writer knows what writer's block is. Not only does the mind go blank, but even the hands seem to refuse to move, the fingers freeze, and it is almost physically impossible to write even a single letter or a meaningless word. The body just does not respond. There is no question of greater or less inspiration, of dull moments and exciting times. This block goes much deeper and closes down all possibilities of writing anything at all on the blank page. The cause of this block can very well be the fear of writing a best-seller in its field and creating a sensation. I can imagine the plight of the writer who writes a best-seller after the first exhilaration has died down. He cannot stop there. He has to write again, he has to produce another work, and this will be inevitably measured against the previous success, only to be declared second-rate by comparison, so that the judgment will hurt and bring pressure. When can I bring out another masterpiece? How can I win back the critics' approval? Has my inspiration died down? Where is my creativity, my power of description and imagination? If I could do it once, why not again? I am the same, as my paper and pen are the same; why, then, can't I warm up again and shake myself into something worthwhile once more? What is missing? What is wrong with me? Have I slumped definitely into mediocrity, or can I still have hopes of reaching other peaks and climbing new summits?

Success brings elation for a start and slavery in its trail. And the fear of that burden may be anonymously present in the mind before action starts and may sabotage it to avoid its tension. Behind self-defeating behavior lurks always the fear of success. A. J. Cronin dumped into the wastepaper basket the manuscript of his first novel, *The*

Citadel, which, rescued on second thought at the last moment, went on to become a best-seller and converted its author from an unknown doctor into a leading novelist. Why the wastebasket? The apparent fear was that no publisher would print the novel, but that could be easily checked by approaching them, and he had not yet asked anyone. Indeed, no one but his wife knew that he was writing a novel. The real fear was that the novel could prove a success and shake him away from his secure life as a doctor into the unpredictable world of writers and readers and publishers.

Such is the battle between mediocrity and excellence, between backstage and limelight, between safety and risk. The adventure is worth it, but many things inside a person shrink from it and boycott the proceedings without his realizing it. Our inborn laziness tries to avoid the strains of an achiever's life by preventing us from entering into it. Thus the fear of success is born in us, and the path to the summit is effectively blocked.

Perfectionism in all its shapes is a clear manifestation of the fear of success. No draft is good enough, no plan will do, no preparation is sufficient. The truth is exactly the opposite. The work in readiness is surely going to be good, indeed too good by any standards, and therefore the fear sets in that once that level of perfection has been publicly attained, it will have to be kept up in every subsequent production. That prospect is worrisome, and to avoid it, the mind plots endless delays and repeated trials. Drafts are rejected with the secret hope that none will ultimately be accepted, and by failing to deliver this time, we shall not be asked at all the next. Drop out in order to avoid tensions, and since the naked dropping out is not respectable, we disguise it under a cloak of perfection. Unless I am satisfied with my own work, I cannot submit it, and since I shall never be satisfied, I will never submit it, only to remain in the barren aloofness of my own fear. Nothing but the best will do for me, and since that best will never be attained, I can remain safe and contented far from all competition. The price of success is heavy, and its apprehensive anticipation can close the door to a success that is at the same time desired and feared. The fact is, we fear success even more than we fear failure; it is only that the fear of failure is open, while the fear of success is hidden. It is to our advantage to be aware of it.

Iris Murdoch bases her long novel *The Book and the Brotherhood* on the not so rare psychological fear that when success is achieved, life will come to an end. A group of intellectual friends have commissioned one of their number to write a book on political theory, which all think will have a great influence on thinking people and will contribute to changing for the better the political scene of the country and the world. "The book that the age requires." A book that will be a philosophical analysis and a program of action "about everything except Aristotle." The writer himself, David Crimond, calls it "a very important book," and dedicates to it all his time and energy through many years. He has no money of his own, and so his friends generously finance the project that he may freely write his book without any worries. The years pass, however, and the book is not forthcoming, so that the members of the financing committee begin to get nervous, and some even doubt Crimond's intentions. Is he stalling so as to keep getting the allowances he knows will stop when he finishes the book?

Crimond reveals the real reason to Jean: "When I finish the book I shall cease to be." And therefore, "Perhaps the book will never be finished." The book was his work, his masterpiece, his life. Once the book is over, life will be over; there will not be anything more to do, nothing more to live for. Irrational fear of a decidedly bright but inwardly tormented man who identifies his lifework with his life and fears his extinction when he completes his work.

The committee urges results, and the book is completed. Even its critics are forced to admit that it is an extraordinary work. "Some will hate it, some will love it. It will be widely read, widely discussed, and very influential." Oxford University Press accepts the book for publication. And then Crimond's fear of success climaxes and he enters into a suicide pact with Jean. They are each to drive in a car at full speed against each other for a head-on collision at dead of night on the Roman Road. The scheme, though carefully rehearsed, fails because Jean swerves at the last moment. Then Crimond tries a pistol duel with Jean's husband, but there also, he fails to be killed. When the novel ends, Crimond is learning Arabic— to write another book. After all, one has to go on living.*

* Iris Murdoch, *The Book and the Brotherhood* (New York: Penguin U.S.A., 1988).

TRAFFIC ON THE ROAD

A woman religious once told me she was afraid of cars on the road. Nothing extraordinary in itself if we take into account the state of our roads and the speed of our cars. But with her it was something of a phobia. She found it difficult to cross a street even at a green light, and to enter the crosswalk without traffic lights was for her a major adventure. There was definitely something behind her fear of cars. It turned out to be fear of people. Moving units on the roads of life. She feared company, feared dialogue, feared encounters of any kind, feared living in a group. Disabling fear for a person who has chosen to live in community with others. In its milder manifestations this fear of people is not uncommon, and it can greatly inhibit personal growth. The sooner it is uncovered, the better.

Fear of people is ultimately fear of being rejected. The human person stands on dignity, and the supreme test is to be accepted as a person, not for any external achievement but for personal worth, or . . . to be rejected. Love is the greatest adventure in life, and therefore it entails the greatest risk, the risk of facing another person in defenseless innocence, opening up without reserve and waiting for a response. Do you want me? The response is never guaranteed, and therein lies its value. With reason or without any reason, out of instinct or feeling, of seasoned judgment or irrational prejudice, the response comes from person to person, and it consecrates a friendship or sets up a wall. This is the final insecurity, as there is no justification, no pleading, no court of appeal, and what is at stake is not my achievements or my qualities, my results or my successes, but I myself as a person, as a friend. To be rejected is the ultimate condemnation. No wonder that in order to avoid such a gloomy possibility, we may at times inhibit ourselves, draw back and choose solitude. But the price of solitude is greater than the pain of rejection.

There are people in group life who keep entirely to themselves, do not come close to anybody, and do not allow anybody to get close to them. Usually such persons will be perfect ladies or gentlemen, polite to a fault and thoughtful without fail. They will never hurt anybody— just in order not to be hurt themselves. They will never forget a birthday or miss an anniversary. They will always use the correct expression and exhibit the exact smile. Their very politeness is a shield to protect themselves from any attempt at intimacy. "Stay where you are. Smile back. Give the standard answer to my standard greeting. Measure your smile according to mine. And don't, for the life of you, try to take any liberties with me. Keep your distance. My handshake is telling you where you belong. Don't trespass over that line. You live your life and I will live mine and all will be fine, but don't mix your life with mine in any way. I stand alone."

There are such loners among us. They prefer affective sterility to emotional insecurity. They do not realize what they miss. If anywhere, it is here that one has to break the frontiers of fear in order to develop and to grow. We develop our minds through study and our bodies through exercise, and we may leave our affectivity stunted, to our own loss. Its exercise is friendship and love, and its reward is the blossoming forth of the best and deepest part of our being in fullness of humanity. If a flower were afraid of the winds and the insects and the hand of a person that can pluck it for pleasure or for gain, it would never open its petals even if the sun tried to persuade it with its warmth; that is, it would never become a flower. To become a flower, it has to open, so that its perfume and its color may enliven the paths of people. The penalty for fear is barrenness. No garden and no beauty. There is risk in flowering, but without the risk, there is no life. The flower eventually lets itself be persuaded into the great adventure, and the world is a better world with flowers.

Part of the male-dominated culture we have inherited is that the proposal to marry is still normally made by the boy, not by the girl. The proposal involves a risk: The other party may say no, may even repeat the old-fashioned formula "You have paid me the greatest compliment a man can pay a woman, and I will remember and honor you to the end of my life, but . . . ," and so the proposing party may be left high and dry to handle his own feelings and his discomfiture before friends and relatives. Maybe it was because of the risk involved that the task of proposing was entrusted to the purportedly stronger member of the species. Let him venture and take the jilt when it comes. The woman will be protected, as she can always say no and wait for the next. A safe position, to be sure, but not exempt of its own difficulties, as I learned in the case of a girl I knew well.

She was very much in love with a certain boy, but she could not bring herself to get from this boyfriend the elementary clarification about his feelings and intentions, much less in India, where the marriage is usually arranged by the parents, and so she was just hoping her parents would see the situation and do the necessary. The boy did not say anything either, and the dangerous game of taking things for granted was played fully on both sides. I warned the girl, but she declared she could do nothing to get an assurance. Her heart was all she had to go by. Beautiful but risky. What she did get in the mail one day after some time was an invitation to a wedding. The bride was unknown to her, but the bridegroom's name was thoroughly familiar: the name of her own boyfriend. She had not dared to ask in time, when a mutual agreement could have earned their parents' blessing and made two young people very happy.

The story has a sad end. The girl never married. She had been hurt once in the most vulnerable tissue of her youth and was not ready to face a similar hurt again. She would remain alone, far from any person or any situation that could threaten her sensibility again. She would keep nursing an old wound to remind herself not to risk new ones. Like the petals of the *mimosa pudica*, she had closed in at the first touch and now refused to open again. A withered life under the very fear of existence.

Another aspect to the fear of being hurt, which results in affective withdrawal, is the fear that if people come close, they will find out things about me that I do not want known, and so once more I erect a defensive, protective wall all around myself. In the last analysis it is low self-esteem that makes the victim believe people will despise him if they know him or the circumstances of his life as they are in reality. Once I asked a bright young man in college, "Who are your friends?" and he looked down and remained silent. There was no one he could call his friend, and he knew it. The reason was painful to admit and had to be handled with utmost sensitivity. He was the only son, his parents had separated, and he lived alone with his mother. Now if he made friends, they would come home and ask questions and eventually find out the situation, which meant shame and suffering for him. To spare himself such humiliation, he kept all at a distance and lived in isolation. He did not realize then the heavy price he was paying for a frail and temporary safety. He was not to blame for his home situation, and companions and coworkers will eventually find out about it and about his anxiety to hide it, which will make matters worse in the future.

It would be much healthier, though difficult for that young man, to realize that there is nothing to hide, let friends in, open heart and home to them, and see himself accepted with all his family problems and personal weaknesses, and live in open relationship with all. My own self-worth remains intact no matter what difficulties are experienced by those who are close to me.

It is true that people at large and young people in particular can be thoughtlessly cruel in their spiteful criticism of others' social situations. But it is also a fact that if the situation is candidly exposed and freely admitted, criticism will subside and acceptance will eventually be won. And in any case, there is no greater calamity than to condemn oneself to total isolation for life. No fear is valid justification for a lonely life.

If we have to be careful with traffic, we have also to be careful with people. Not any driving will do on any road. We have to study character and circumstance to judge whom we want close to us and whom at a distance. Indeed, a sense of distance is one of the most important instincts we can develop for a happy social life. The point here is not to make the distance so great for all that no one is allowed to come close and we remain aloof. Nobody ever bloomed by standing aloof.

OF GHOSTS AND FEVERS

When I mentioned the practical rule, with due balance of mind and constant common sense, that "if you are afraid of it, do it," I implied that in practice, most fears are only imaginary. Their shadow is longer than their true measure. When we face a fear and call its bluff, it usually dissolves into nothingness, leaving us with the relief of the burden removed and the wistful realization of our temporary stupidity in trembling before a nonexisting threat. We learn courage by challenging fears.

Our boarders in the college hostel believe unanimously in the existence of ghosts. Back in their villages in the Indian countryside, they have grown up close to the village ghosts, with their legends, their claims, and their deeds witnessed by all generations in ready tradition of credulous fear. When they come to town, they bring with them their familiar atmosphere, and soon their ghosts populate our neighborhood. There is an old, abandoned well in our grounds, an ideal dwelling place for a companionable ghost, and right enough, our boys at once declared it to be the abode of the ghost. It was seen by several boys on successive nights in different places, and no one dared approach the well in which it hid during the day. A coconut and a few coins were thrown into the well to the accompaniment of incantations to placate the ghost and prevent its interference in our life. I did not quite understand what a ghost could do with a coconut and coins till I saw the next day a few urchins climbing down the well with utter disregard for any curse. Maybe they were in collusion with the ghost and profited by its demands. The management had only feared that the ghost's presence could reach some rooms or even a whole wing in the hostel, in which case no student could be persuaded to occupy any of those rooms. But the demand for hostel rooms was very high, and that must have kept the ghost out of bounds, or out of the students' imagination in those quarters and for their own interest.

I asked a Hindu friend who was looking for a suitable young man to marry his daughter to, "Will you ask for his horoscope and see whether it is compatible with your daughter's horoscope for a happy marriage?" He answered, "Yes. I personally do not believe that the position of the stars at a person's birth has anything to do with his happiness in marriage, but I am afraid that if anything goes wrong afterwards in their married life, everybody will blame me for not having made sure that their horoscopes matched, and so I definitely intend making sure they do." For safety's sake. Just in case. The irrational fear that any enlightened person recognizes has no basis, and to which, all the same, many enlightened persons submit out of social pressure or inward uneasiness. Another friend of mine refused to perform the customary ceremonies to placate the spirits of the grounds on which he was to build his new house. The house was built, and shortly after he moved into it with his family, his small daughter fell facedown in a shallow pool of water on the grounds, and was drowned. All his neighbors were unanimous in their verdict. He had offended the spirits, and they had taken revenge. He never believed such a thing, but the pain of his daughter's loss was made heavier by his neighbors' lack of understanding.

Black magic is a source of fear which to a Western mind
is difficult to understand, but which causes untold suffering and misery to many people even today. It is the
conviction that another person can bring evil on me by
performing certain rites and incantations on my name, my
photograph, or an image of me, or just by looking at me
with an evil eye. Many trucks on the Indian roads carry on
their back fenders an inscription against the evil eye. The
fear is that any person who sees a large truck loaded with
goods may feel jealous of it and may utter a curse and
provoke an accident. To forestall such a danger, the driver
inscribes at the back of his truck a sentence to counteract
the evil eye, and that anticurse takes, curiously, two
opposite forms. One is a countercurse to discourage the
first curse: "If you are jealous, may you get a black face";
and the other, refreshingly, is a blessing to ward off, as
with a shield, the evil looks: "My blessings on your
jealousy!" Thus the long-suffering truck drivers protect
themselves and their trucks from the hazards of the road
and of human envy.

Indian women perform a delicate ritual every morning
in which devotion and beauty combine to embellish their
sleek foreheads. After the face is washed and the hair
combed, they place a round red mark in the middle of
their foreheads as the closing gesture of their toilettes to be
ready for the day. The mark is a good luck mark, a beauty
spot, a sign in a married woman that her husband is alive,
a seal of protection on the thoughts that will cross behind
it during the day, a consecration of the whole body to God
in devout submission. What many do not know, even the
women who faithfully perform the morning ritual, is that
primarily and originally the red spot is supposed to be a
protection against the evil eye. High on the woman's
forehead, it will protect her, like Shiva's third eye, deflect-

ing to itself any look of jealousy or dangerous attraction to the beautiful face, and absorbing it and rendering it harmless before it may cause any damage. A beauty spot to protect beauty.

Ashes are sacred in India. They are given by holy men to convey blessings, and their contempt could bring down divine displeasure on thoughtless unbelievers. Here is a little experience with sacred ashes conveyed by Harindra Dave, poet, novelist, and editor of a Bombay daily. "Three friends, Parmanand Kapadia, Ghanshyam Desai, and I, were coming out of a public lecture when we saw a holy man, a *sadhu*, dressed in saffron and surrounded by people. None of us knew who he was, and so Parmanand, with his characteristic curiosity to know everybody who could mean something in Bombay, approached him at once, and came back after speaking briefly with him. He told us, 'He is a wandering *sadhu* who goes about giving people holy ashes as a sign of God's favor. See,' he said, showing us his hand and opening it, 'he has given me this handful of ashes. I don't believe in this, so take them and keep them if you or anybody in your house believes in them.' And with that, he put the ashes in my hand. I was taken by surprise, and did not know what to do with them. Seeing my predicament, Ghanshyam took them from me and threw them in a garbage bin. Here is where faith, superstition, and fear combine. Parmanand did not believe in the ashes, yet he was afraid something unpleasant could happen to him if he showed disrespect to them. I have religious faith, but I could not bring myself to keep the ashes nor to throw them. Ghanshyam was not a pious man nor an atheist either, but he had not the least scruple to dispose of the embarrassing ashes in the simplest way. And the three of us were hardened intellectuals in a sophisticated city!"

Another Indian writer, Anil Joshi, tells another personal experience of ashes and guilt. "When I was a boy there was once a fair in my village, and I was impatient to go and see it. I was leaving the house when my mother shouted at me: 'Before going to the fair, light the oil lamp before the image of Krishna. Here are the matches. First bow to the image and then go.' I took the matchbox in a hurry, opened the niche where the little statue was, placed there the oil lamp, and lit it. With a half bow and a full jump I was out on the street and on to the fair. It was the fair held to commemorate every year the birth of Krishna, and I had the whole day now to enjoy it. The lamp I had lit at home was the daily morning rite, to place a burning light before the sacred image for daylong protection, and now I had the whole day to enjoy myself at the fair. I did so and returned home in the evening, tired like a deflated balloon. On entering our neighborhood, I noticed something strange in the air. I reached home, and all were serious and silent. In the middle of the room they had placed a vessel with milk, and inside it I saw the statue of Krishna. I understood. I looked at the niche, and it was burned. In my hurry I had not placed the oil lamp properly, and it had burnt all to ashes. Gone were Krishna's crown and his peacock feather, and the statue itself was blackened, and that was why it had now been placed in cold milk as a therapeutic pious gesture to heal the burns on the flesh of God. And I was responsible for it. When I saw the ashes I felt guilty, and I could not sleep that night. It is well known that Krishna is represented with dark skin, but since that unhappy day I have always believed that his color is dark because I burned him. Since then I have been afraid of fire and ashes."

I learned more about fears and incantations and magic during a visit to Africa. While visiting a factory in an

African capital, I turned to one of the workers, and in what to me was a friendly gesture, I asked him his name. He did not answer and turned the other way. I naively thought he may not have understood my English, but after the visit was over, my host explained to me the mistake I had made. "Here you must never ask an unknown person his name," he said. "If he gives you his real name, you acquire power over him, as you can use his name to bring evil upon him with magic practices." I remembered then having read a similar story about American Indians, and recalled that we in the West also would not give our name and address to a stranger.

I heard more in Africa. When people go from their villages to a city hospital for a serious illness or an operation, it seems to be common practice not to give their real names and addresses, but fictitious ones. The reasoning behind this is that if the fever, once it has forcibly been made to leave the body by the strength of the medicines, learns the name and address of the person who was sick, it will find its way to his village, seek him out, and stick again to him with greater violence than before. So they register under a wrong name to put the fever off and cut the trail. One can never take enough precautions.

Rudyard Kipling, who knew well the ways of Indian peasants and holy men, noticed the same belief among them. When the Jat brings his sick child to Kim, he says: "I have walked the pillars and trodden the temples till my feet are flayed, and the child is no whit better. We changed his name when the fever came. We put him into girl's clothes. There was nothing we did not do. I am at my very wits' end." Again the changing of the name to cheat the fever, and even dressing the boy as a girl for further disguise. These were the common practices among simple people when sickness came, and all had been duly tried.

Then came ceremonies in temples and blessings by holy men, but nothing had availed. It was Kim, the Friend of all the World, who with his Eastern compassion and Western training found the remedy for the child's malaria in a few quinine tablets. And the lama, whom he serves, praises him: "To heal the sick is to acquire merit. That was wisely done, O Friend of all the World."*

There is a tendency in humans to deify that which we fear. The Greeks deified thunder in the hands of Zeus, and sea storms in the might of Poseidon's trident. An ancient scourge in India was smallpox, and it became a goddess, Shitala. Curiously enough, and as an expression of the same paradox, her name means the opposite of what she is supposed to be. Symptoms of smallpox are the heat it generates in the body and the craterlike pustules that erupt all over the skin, and Shitala means "the Cool One." Coolness to signify fever, and a goddess to represent a deadly disease. It is a triumph of modern science that smallpox has been entirely eradicated from India. But the temples and images of the smallpox goddess remain as witnesses and reminders of man's tendency to sublimate his fears. We do not worship Zeus or Shitala anymore, but we do sometimes put religious labels on human fears and escape into rationalization instead of directly facing the menace. Such a treatment covers up the fear but does not heal the soul. Quinine is better.

Albert Schweitzer knew the extent of the fear of black magic among the people he worked with from his hospital in Lambaréné, and came to see his mission as an attempt to liberate them from the dark fear of imaginary spirits. He wrote:

---

* Rudyard Kipling, *Kim*, in *Rudyard Kipling Illustrated* (New York: Crown, 1982), 715.

Besides the fear of poisons there is the fear inspired
by the inimical supernatural power a man can bring
to bear on another. The aboriginals believe there are
means by which a man can obtain mastery over magic
forces. He who obtains a powerful fetish can do
everything. He is lucky when hunting, becomes rich,
and can bring calamity, sickness and even death to
those he wants to harm. A European will never be
able to understand how horrible the life of these
people is, living as they do day by day in fear of the
fetishes that can be used against them. The cult of the
fetish is a product of fear in primitive man. He wants
to acquire a charm that may be able to protect him
against the inimical spirits of the dead, of nature and
of the wicked power of other men. Only a person that
has seen such misery at close quarters will realize that
it is a duty on humankind to bring to these peoples
new ideas about the world and about life in order to
liberate them from those absurd beliefs that torture
them.*

What Schweitzer does not seem to have realized, as he
speaks of the misery of primitive man without paying
attention to the misery of civilized man, is that without all
the trappings of the fears of the jungle aboriginal, Western
man too is full of fears and superstitions that darken his
mind and cripple his action. In a way, the fear of the
material fetish is less harmful because the object can be
pointed out, uncovered, and discredited, and the fear
shown groundless; whereas the unspoken fear that comes
from hidden complexes and dark assumptions and that
works secretly on our minds is much harder to identify
and expose. Our fetishes are more subtle and therefore

* Albert Schweitzer, *Zwischen Wasser und Urwald* (Buenos Aires: Libraria
Hachette, S.A., 1956), 51, 53.

much more dangerous: fear of being hurt by others, when
in true fact only we can hurt ourselves; fear of losing social
esteem, when we know well such a social esteem is not
worth caring for; fear of hidden diseases or sudden heart
attacks which, yes, may definitely occur, but which fear
cannot keep away (and, in fact, brings closer). Hidden
fears, dark apprehensions, sudden fright. There are large
shadows over our lives, and we uneasily wind our way
through them, not knowing what may befall us next. Fear
of our surroundings prevents us from contemplating the
landscape and enjoying the journey. Only a fearless
existence will do full justice to our human birth. We can
learn to diminish our fears by the simple procedure of
facing them.

One of my favorite walks in the sacred wilderness of
Mount Abu in Rajasthan is to the vivid, transparent,
almost musically alive waters of Trevor Tal, the secluded
lake, high among sharp mountain peaks, far from any
human habitation, meeting point of wild game under the
silent moon, partner and accomplice of my solo swims in
Paradise Regained. One day in the early morning I
started for the lake, left behind the township, the
temples, the fields that bore the mark of the presence of
man, and turned left to take the mountain path I knew so
well. But then something stopped me. Right in the
middle of the only path to the lake stood a soldier, armed
to the teeth, with unsheathed bayonet fixed to the barrel
of his gun, the butt of which he rested on the ground
while he barred with his open legs the way to any
trespasser. I understood. The army was out for maneuvers
in that part of the mountains, and civilian walkers were
barred as an elementary precaution. I thought it wise to
avoid a confrontation with the Indian army, and turned
quietly back. Trevor Tal can wait for another day. There

are other paths on the mountain in other directions, and any of them will be my route for the day.

I was in fact moving away in the opposite direction when a thought struck me. Why not try Trevor Tal after all? Nothing is lost by asking. The soldier is there, right enough, but I haven't asked him. He is not likely to use his bayonet on me if I inquire politely. Let me see. I approached him straight, and asked him directly, "Is this the way to Trevor Tal?" On hearing my question, the soldier, to my amusement, clicked his heels, stood to attention, jerked his right hand to his forehead in salute to me, and intoned militarily, "Yes, sir!" Then he turned aside and saluted again as I walked past him into the mountain. I saluted back, stood tall, and marched on. My fear had been groundless. Whatever else that soldier was doing on that spot, he was definitely not there to stop peaceful walkers. I went on to Trevor Tal under army protection in a spotless morning. After all, I mused while I walked, the army is there to protect us, not to frighten us. And is it not the same with all our imaginary fears along the paths of life? Let them not spoil our walk.

LET THE WORST HAPPEN

When we cannot face bodily the object of our fears, we can always do it mentally. We can say to ourselves gently and pointedly when the thought of impending disaster rises in our minds: All right, it is going to happen, and . . . so what? These last two words can be a truly magic formula: So what? A religious sister once confided to me that those two little words were her trusted key to peace of mind and quietness of life. She was leading a rather eventful existence, and had to face small and big crises almost every day under a tension that would have broken a lesser soul. Her way to strengthen herself when calamity threatened was to tell herself quietly and directly: Yes, I know the worst, and it is going to happen; so what? Her experience was that with that little exercise, the pressure diminished greatly or disappeared entirely—until the next occasion, of course.

There are reasons for it. The anticipated fear is enhanced with all the terrors a wild imagination can lend it, and that at a time when the organism does not muster the necessary defenses against it, simply because the occasion is not yet present. When the feared event actually takes place, all the resources of nature and grace will be brought to bear on the situation, obstacles will be overcome, and victory will be obtained or, in the worst case, defeat will become bearable. In the actual crisis we always find we have greater strength than in the anticipated nightmare. The coward dies a thousand deaths; the courageous hero may die, but only once. When we run away from danger, we increase our perception of it and its burden on our imagination. When, on the contrary, we turn and face it, even if only in our minds, it is cut down to size and becomes manageable. I am afraid I am going to fail in the examination. All right, I am going to fail. So what? I'm not likely to die because of that. The worst that may happen is that I lose a year in my studies. That looks very big now, but once I am out of this and get working, who will care whether I took one year more or one year less to finish my studies? People will forget, as I myself will forget with the passage of time. What today looks like an insurmountable obstacle, very soon will fade into insignificance. Gain perspective and lose fear. Or yes, I am going to get myself examined for this rather stubborn pain that does not leave me, and I know from this point, it is going to be cancer. So I'm going to have cancer. Fine. There are treatments and things to be done about it. I am not the first cancer patient in the world. I know quite a few, and some seem to be almost unconcerned, and some actually get cured. Many things can happen still. And finally, let's take the ultimate: Yes, I'm going to die. So what? Is that news? Everybody dies sooner or later, and again, a few years this way or that may look impressive now, but in the last analysis, they do not make any great difference. I know I'm going to die, and I say it plainly before everybody. In a way, that is the ultimate peace. Nobody is likely to disturb me now, and I can look forward to a distinguished funeral.

This may look like making light of real fears, but that is precisely what happens when we tackle those fears with the "so what?" approach. We finally see their ludicrous side, the lack of proportion, the fun of it all, and we laugh at ourselves. Then the fear dissolves. On the other hand, this is no universal remedy, and does not pretend in any case to diminish the reality of suffering or make light of real sorrows in life. There are situations where it would be tactless or even offensive to ask unconcernedly, So what? We have to respect suffering and not laugh at the plight of others when we feel safe. The "so what?" advice is not to be proferred patronizingly before a burdened soul. If not properly used, the victim could reply: "You tell me that because you are not under the same threat. If you were in my place, you would keep your clever advice to yourself. It is easy to advise others, but wait till you get into trouble, and then you'll tell me whether you can easily say, So what?" Prudence and sensitivity are never to be forgotten when we deal with others, and even with ourselves. If we cannot heal suffering, let us at least not make it worse.

Yet this sprightly approach works also in some unlikely cases. I have met several persons in my life, not many, but again, not altogether few, who are genuinely afraid, and some somberly convinced, that they are irremediably condemned to go to hell for all eternity. It seems impossible that pious persons should consider themselves damned forever, but a misguided education, early fears, and persistent scruples can cause havoc in a docile mind and lead to despair. Such cases are not easy to deal with, as the afflicted person attributes every effort to help him to the kindness of the helper, but he knows his own misery and does not let go easily. It would seem that the last thing one could tell any such person would be "Well, well, I understand that you are going to hell forever. So what?" The reaction may be stronger than anticipated and may make matters worse.

Still, well advised or not, I once tried the approach with a saintly woman religious who, according to her, was irrevocably on her way to eternal damnation. "You tell me you are damned to hell. Let it be true. So what?" She had been quite serious through all the painful dialogue, but when it came to this point, she burst out laughing in spite of herself, and there was no need of further discussion on the matter. She saw, when confronted with the straight admission of her madness, how impossible and absurd her proposition was, and then it struck her that the only sane thing to do before such derangement was to laugh. The little question "So what?" brought a touch of realism to a mind that, in that particular point, had deviated from all logic and common sense and saw itself caught in the vicious grip of a self-deprecating pessimism. Back to reality is the formula to allay all fears and restore balance. What actually happens is never so dreadful as what was long feared. We have greater power of endurance than we ourselves think. Nature is wise and God is great, and there is always a way out of every trial, a solution to every problem, or at least the personal effort to cope with life as it comes to us day by day. Once we accept the worst, anything else is bound to appear as a relief.

Buddha instructed his disciples, "People when seeing you and listening to you may insult you and say ill things of you." They acknowledged the teaching and said, "Yes, people when seeing us will insult us and say ill things of us." Buddha continued, "They will also throw stones at you and hurt you." They replied, "We know it; people will throw stones at us and hurt us." Buddha insisted, "People may get so angry at you that they may attack you and kill you." And the same quiet answer came from the disciples, "Yes, people will get angry at us and attack us and kill us." That was the sacred message to make all fears recede and all courage build up, so that the disciples could travel far and wide in the service of their creed.

There was a courageous queen in Persian Iraq in the

tenth century who seemed to have used the same tactics of expecting the worst and saying so in order to become fearless in rather delicate and dangerous circumstances for her throne. Queen Seada's husband had died, and her son was still a minor, so that she had to rule the country as a regent. Now, Sultan Mahmud of Gazna, the Idol-Breaker, who had extended his conquests up to Indian soil, had an eye on those territories, and when the king died, he decided to annex them to his already vast kingdom. To find an excuse for the invasion, he wrote to Queen Seada, demanding heavy tributes. As she would not be able to pay, neither to defend her land before a greatly superior army, a quick invasion would settle the matter. The queen knew the danger, envisaged the worst, and wrote accordingly to the threatening invader: "While my husband was alive I was in fear of the great king Mahmud, who has overrun Persia and India. Now I have no fear. I know that such a monarch would never send an army to combat a woman. If he were to fight me, I would resist to the end. If I were to win, I would be renowned for evermore. But if the Sultan Mahmad were to prevail—men would merely say that he had defeated an old woman. Because I realise that the Sultan is too wise a man to lay himself open to either of these alternatives, I am not afraid of what may happen."* The letter had the desired effect, and the sultan never invaded the queen's domains.

Accepting my fears is the way to become fearless. Knowledge of my weakness is my main strength.

---

* Idries Shah, *Caravan of Dreams* (London, Octagon Press, Ltd., 1988), 137.

INNOCENCE AND GUILT

G. K. Chesteron expressed well the burden of original sin when he saw it reflected in the fact that, whatever people are, they are not quite what they were supposed to be. Something has gone wrong, something is missing, something has been twisted out of shape, and we daily experience, in ourselves and in others, the lopsided view, the limping gait, the incomplete result in our best efforts and most genuine desires. Something in us needs healing, needs others' patience and God's pardon, and without that dark reality of sin in the world, we cannot explain our lives and cannot explain human history. That fact is clear, and is the basis of our religious experience as imperfect people under a loving God.

It is also equally clear, however, that the fact of our sinfulness is at times exaggerated by our own morbidity against ourselves, and against others, by the recurring temptation to manipulate them into subservience through a sense of guilt. As guilt has much to do with fear, it is important to regain the balance and not be drawn to moral pessimism on one side or to irresponsible levity on the other. God is a Father, and we'll do well to allow this basic and consoling truth to become a practical principle in our lives.

The fact that I had exaggerated guilt in my life (and, unwittingly, contributed guilt in the lives of others through my preachings and retreats) was brought home to me with a smile while watching an entertaining movie, *The Gods Must Be Crazy*. It depicts the adventures of a group of Bushmen in Africa who have found in their jungle an empty bottle of Coca-Cola, dropped carelessly by a pilot who had flown over their land. The main actor was actually a Bushman who acted with unrehearsed spontaneity and vanished into the jungle after the shooting before they could pay him, and could not be found when, after the success of the picture, a sequel was planned with the same cast. He had no use for money, in any case, in the simplicity of his life and the straightforwardness of his concepts.

The relevant episode here is the one in which our candid Bushman, under the spell of the empty bottle, wanders into a modern city and faces traffic, crowds, and policemen. He feels hungry in the unfriendly city and tries to satisfy his hunger in the only way he knows. He has spotted a goat, goes near it, caresses it, asks its pardon in the traditional way for having to kill it in order to survive, and kills it. The trouble is that the goat has an owner, a concept our Bushman does not understand, and the owner complains, the police intervene, and our man goes to court to be judged. The judge, after listening to the evidence, requests of the lawyer, who also acts as interpreter, "Ask the accused whether he pleads guilty or not guilty." The lawyer hesitates for a moment, turns to the judge instead of turning to the Bushman, and says respectfully, "Sir, in the language of these people there is no word for 'guilty.' "

There are occasions when the time wasted in seeing a movie is fully redeemed, and for me this was one of them. I mused on the implications of that innocent fact. One need not be a linguist to realize that if a word for a concept is entirely missing in a language, the concept is also missing. Language reflects culture. The Eskimos have a dozen words to say "snow" while we manage with one, because the different types of snow are important for them and not for us. And in the languages of India there are different words for "father's brother," "father's sister's husband," "mother's brother," and "mother's sister's husband," who are all "uncles" in English, a reminder that family ties are stronger and subtler in India than in Europe. Those good Bushmen, then, literally did not know what "guilt" was. The word was not in their vocabulary because the concept was not in their minds. Blessed people! Whatever their philosophy or their lack of it, they did not consider themselves liable to moral guilt. There must be transgressions, irregularities, mistakes in their conduct, which the tribe will check and even punish, but the idea of personal accountability for moral evil was definitely absent from the conceptual world. A nagging thought occurred to me then: How did the first Christian missionaries manage to convey their essential message to those people? Jesus is for us the Redeemer who becomes one of us and justifies us before the Father with his love and his sufferings unto death. For people who did not see themselves as sinners, it must have been difficult to understand the notion of a redeemer. What this means for me in a positive way is that Africa has much to contribute to the understanding and loving of the person of Christ when its peoples can think freely and originally from their own culture instead of having a foreign outlook imposed on them. Any one continent has much to learn from all the others.

Another illuminating example comes from Africa. Baroness Karen Blixen, who in many ways came to sympathize deeply and understand personally the ways of Africa, experienced difficulty nonetheless on certain points, and one of them was precisely this question of moral guilt. She recounts in *Out of Africa* an incident that occurred in the village near her coffee plantation which brought the point home to her. Some children were playing with firearms they had taken from their homes, when a rifle in the hands of one of them accidentally went off with such ill fortune that the bullet hit another boy in the group, who died on the spot. The case came up before the village elders for judgment, and the baroness, as acknowledged head of the village, presided over the deliberations. The main point in her Western (or, shall we say here, "Northern") mind was to establish beyond doubt whether the mishap had truly been an accident, or whether there was any kind of intention and therefore culpability on the part of the boy who held the gun.

Her questioning went on for some time, till she realized she was making no headway. None in the group of elders around her was following her reasoning. Finally they made their point clear to her. They said something like this: "We do not know what you mean when you insist in finding out whether there was any intention, culpability, or responsibility on the part of the first boy. We only know that the gun was in his hands and he fired it and the other boy was killed. What we are here now for is to determine the amount of the damage caused to the father of the boy who died and who relied on his son for his future, and consequently to fix the number of cows, sheep, and goats the father of the boy who fired the gun has to pay to the father of the boy who was killed. Let us do that, and our work is over." The baroness understood. There was no question of finding out, as a European court would, whether the boy was guilty or not; that was not the issue at all because, again, the concept of moral guilt was not part of their mental makeup. Count the goats, and the job is done.

The baroness drew a conclusion from these experiences which is at variance with the opinion of Albert Schweitzer, quoted earlier, and which also deserves consideration. The Africans, she concludes, are less afraid than the Europeans. "The Natives have, far less than the white people, a sense of risks in life. Sometimes on a Safari, or on the farm, in a moment of extreme tension, I have met the eyes of my Native companions, and have felt that we were at a great distance from one another, and that they were wondering at my apprehension of our risk. It made me reflect that perhaps they were, in life itself, within their own element, such as we can never be, like fishes in deep water which for the life of them cannot understand our fear of drowning."[*]

Oneness with nature, and innocence of outlook, make for minimum fear and maximum confidence in living our lives. I encountered the same attitude in the college students I met and lived with when I first went to study the Gujarati language as a boarder on the campus of an Indian university. In our discussions, which for me were invaluable experiences not only to practice the language but to learn the mentality of the people I wanted to love and understand, they asked me about Christian ideas, and when I inevitably mentioned sin, they soon noticed the distance that separated us. They were good boys who did not mean harm to anybody and whose point of view in this delicate matter they obligingly repeated until it became clear to me. They accepted limitations, failures, errors, mistakes, frictions, and misunderstandings that could certainly give rise to estrangement and suffering, but they consistently rejected the thought that a "bad"

* Isak Dinesen, *Out of Africa* (London: Century Publishing Co., Ltd., 1985), 20.

action could be performed out of "malice" with a "sinful" conscience.

A professor on the campus, who one day joined our circle, put it more technically: "Sin as a ritual impurity or as a metaphysical limitation, yes; as a moral guilt, no." They all agreed with me, however, that something was wrong with man as we know him, with ourselves as we know ourselves, and that often we find ourselves doing what we do not mean to do and irrationally hurting those we love. Saint Paul's text, "The good which I want to do, I fail to do; but what I do is the wrong which is against my will," has an exact parallel in Duryodhan's lament in the Mahabharata: "I know what is good, yet I don't do it; and I hate what is evil, yet I do it."

We seem fundamentally to share the same experience, and we can learn to temper our different approaches by learning from our different traditions. Here is where the meeting of East and West, and North and South, can be redeemingly enriching for people on all continents.

SEX AND MATHEMATICS

Our conscience is particularly vulnerable when sex is involved. A persistent tradition and a repeated insistence on the part of teachers and moralists ever since our youth have heightened our sensitivity and sharpened our guilt under the weight of shame. We have grown to be afraid of our bodies, of each other, of look and touch, in a world of lust. All other sins in the standard catalogs were either too small to weigh us down, as lying or gossiping, or too big for us to commit them, like murder or looting. Sex was the one sin easy to commit and grievous enough to burden our consciences and make us fear hell. No wonder sex has dominated the moral scene for centuries, and only now are we learning to regain balance and correct perspectives in responsible maturity.

When I was a young religious, a holy old priest who was an international authority on canon law and moral matters visited our house, and we young people were invited to meet him privately in order to benefit from his knowledge and wisdom. I went dutifully, knocked at the door, entered the room, and sat down on the chair across the table in front of him. Before I could say a word or even give my name in self-introduction, he started speaking. His very first words were on sex, and on sex he continued to talk for the twenty minutes or so I remained in his room. I had not asked any question, had not uttered a word. I had thought of only a couple of general questions to ask, and was not prepared for the purposeful onslaught against my shyness. I remained silent through the old man's lecture. He was projecting onto me, as I now realize, his own sex complexes, which were not a few, and deriving satisfaction from talking on the forbidden subject with an innocent audience. Since we were more than a hundred young men in that house, and many visited him, the good old man must have had a great time. So much for his international reputation.

The obsession with sex was common, and thrived on our worst instincts: shame, guilt, and fear. I cannot help the feeling that in the hands of some counselors and directors of the past, sex became, consciously or unconsciously, a tool to manipulate docile souls into ready subservience. Sex induces guilt, guilt breeds fear, and fear can be used to shape into conformity the most rebellious mind. This could explain their reluctance to release the grip on sex and the exaggerated importance they systematically gave to it. While we had to seek guidance and absolution for our sex offenses, they were sure to remain in demand and exert influence as indispensable teachers and judges of our behavior. If sex, as a moral subject, would lose its importance, they would lose their ascendancy as masters of souls. And so sex was exaggerated out of all proportion and made in practice the center of morality. We were made to feel sick so that the hospital would remain full.

This was not always so. Without dreaming of utopia or going back to the all too short spell of innocence in Paradise before original sin, we know times and cultures where the body was not an enemy, and sex not a taboo. We are not angels, to be sure, and there will always be dangers and allurements and falls, and sex continues to be a mighty power that may go wild, break all bounds, and

cause havoc in men's lives; but precisely because of the
forbidding image we have of the negative aspect of sex,
we can benefit by glancing briefly at the spontaneous,
transparent, disarming innocence some people unself-
consciously display as nature's healthy children before the
reality of sex. I choose an example from my mathematical
background.

Bhaskaracharya is the name of the greatest mathematical
genius in Indian history. His best-known work, the *Lilavati*, was written at the beginning of the twelfth century.
The name of the book is strangely poetical, and indeed the
whole volume is written in verse. *Lila* is the Sanskrit word
for "game," "play," "sport," and is even applied to the
divine sport of creation on the playgrounds of nature. And
Lilavati is the feminine proper noun for "the Playful
One," favorite name for a lovely child, a beloved daughter.
Such was Bhaskaracharya's only child, and the story of
how her name came to be on the title page of her father's
treatise is a pathetic legend in Indian tradition. Her
wedding was being planned, and the most important
point, which was the fixing of the exact auspicious moment at which the "joining of the hands" could only take
place, was attended to by her father himself in a way
worthy of his fame and imagination. He bored a calculated
hole in a large lotus leaf, so that water would flow gently
in, and the moment the leaf sank would signal the astral
conjunction that alone made the wedding possible. (I have
seen, in modern India, the officiating Brahmans, in a more
prosaic way but with the same intent, consult with full
attention their wristwatches for the predestined instant.
No looseness can be risked in such a serious matter.)

The ceremony began, the leaf was sinking, and nobody
noticed a small pearl that had broken loose from the bride's
necklace, and slid onto the privileged leaf, and had stopped

up the little precarious hole on the green surface. The ceremony went on. All eyes turned gradually toward the leaf, and all watched and waited. Someone began to suspect. Anything gone wrong? The leaf is not sinking! The water was examined, the pearl was found . . . and all realized with utter consternation that it was already too late. The unique moment had flown away and the wedding could no longer take place. The bejeweled bride was condemned to unmarried existence. It was then, to console his daughter in her grief, that the great master did the only thing he could do. He told her, "I will write a book that will last through ages, and will put your name to it. You will become immortal." How far the father's scholarship healed the daughter's sorrow, we do not know, but the book is there with the name of the hapless girl on its cover: Lilavati.

A mathematics book contains results in the form of theorems, and exercises in the shape of problems. These problems, though essentially abstract calculations, are usually couched in everyday life terms, and thus give us a valuable glimpse into the cultural life of society in that time and country. The problems I solved at school were worded in terms of trains, rivers, towers, or football games. For example, "Find the point on the side of a football field which subtends the largest angle at the opposite goal (thus making shooting more favorable)." No football player will make such calculations, but to propose a problem in terms of greater probability for a goal does help to get the attention of the students in class. Today mathematics textbooks present problems about space travel and computer logic. The cultural environment is reflected in the daily classwork. In this context it is interesting to see which kind of situations were encountered in twelfth-century India. Here are samples from the *Lilavati*:

A peacock is perched on a column nine cubits high. At the foot of the column is a cobra's hole. The peacock sees the snake at a distance three times the height of the column, crawling towards its hole, and dives to catch it. If the speed of the peacock is the same as the speed of the cobra, find at once, O you worthy scholar, the distance from the base of the column to the point at which the peacock catches the snake. [Answer: 12 cubits]

A king gives gifts to brahmins for fifteen days. The first day he gives them four gold coins, the second nine, and so every day five more than the previous one. How many coins does he give on the whole? [Answer: 585]

The god Shankar [another name for Shiva] holds ten attributes in his ten hands: noose, goad, cobra, drum, skull, trident, sceptre, dagger, arrow, bow. If we combine all those attributes in all possible ways in his ten hands, how many different images of the god Shankar can we produce? And if you, O worthy scholar, happen to be a devotee of god Vishnu, how many images of him can you depict with all the combinations of his four attributes, conch, wheel, mace, lotus? [Answer: 3,628,800 for Shankar, and 24 for Vishnu. And now, watch for the next one.]

While a courtesan is making love to her lover her pearl necklace snaps broken. One fifth of the pearls fall on the bed, one third on the floor, one sixth remain on her body, and one tenth in her lover's hands. If six pearls were left threaded in the necklace, how many pearls were there on the whole?

Other examples follow on the number of arrows Arjuna needed to subdue Karna in the Mahabharata battle, on lakes and lotuses and clouds and birds. And in the midst of them all, without provoking any stir or causing an eyebrow to rise, blending with the landscape and flowing with the current, stands the tale of the courtesan and her lover. Sex must have been quite a commonplace occurrence in those days when it can be mentioned so matter-of-factly in a learned treatise.

I have written several mathematics textbooks (including the first treatise on modern abstract algebra in any Indian language), and I can imagine the hue and cry that would have been raised if I had included in any of them a problem like the following: "A prostitute is making love to a client. If the sum of their ages is fifty, and the difference ten, and the woman is younger than the man, find their respective ages." The scandal would have been enormous, the book would have been banned, and I declared a corrupter of youth and made to drink hemlock, as is customary in such cases. I would have never gotten away with it. Yet Bhaskaracharya did. I have before me an old edition of the *Lilavati* with drawings for each example, though, of course, I am not reproducing them here. I am in no way defending prostitution, but I do find it irresistibly refreshing to see sex mentioned nonchalantly together with lotuses and peacocks and kings and gods by a senior scholar and loving father in a treatise inscribed to his virgin daughter. No titillation, no prudery, no Pharisaic scandal, no Victorian taboo.

In twelfth-century India, sex seems to have been taken uneventfully for granted. Moralists like the old man I mentioned at the beginning of the chapter would lose their jobs in such a society. And that would be to everybody's advantage. We can well do without meddlesome casuists. There will always be dangers to guard ourselves from, as there will always be attitudes to learn and balance

to be regained and refined. Avoiding the two extremes
that stalk our path in moral matters, license and scruple,
we can clarify our views and strengthen our stand. We can
learn to build up a responsible reaction to an ancestral
instinct, and sail clear of the complex of shame and guilt
that has long been associated with our bodies. We need
not and should not be afraid of ourselves. Back to sanity.

The answer to the problem is readily found. One-fifth of
the pearls plus one-third plus one-sixth plus one-tenth
plus six pearls equals the total number, which we call x.
That is,

$$\frac{x}{5} + \frac{x}{3} + \frac{x}{6} + \frac{x}{10} + 6 = x$$

Clearing up the fractions and solving for the unknown, we
find the number of pearls to be thirty.

MANIPULATION THROUGH FEAR

Fear opens us to manipulation. I have mentioned that idea and I want to enlarge on it. It is one of the aspects of fear that harms us most, as it erodes our personality and mortgages our freedom. Fear makes us feel insecure, and in our insecurity we readily turn to whatever can make us feel safe again. We are impatient with insecurity, we cannot bear being long in a state of uncertainty, and we rush to protection and clarity at whatever cost. When we feel secure, we can defend our position and stand our ground. We know where we stand, we appreciate other points of view, but we prefer our own for perfectly valid reasons which we know and are ready to expose with quiet confidence. We are even ready to change our opinion and accept other views precisely because we are secure and do not feel threatened by differences or novelties. But if we change, we do so out of our own initiative and volition. Security gives us firmness to stand and to walk as we freely desire. Fear makes us shake, in our minds more than in our bodies, and so we grab at the first prop that may steady our faltering stand. In our weakness we fall an easy prey to any dispenser of certainties. Safety first. And, sadly, independence last.

As a teacher, I know the infallible way to make reluctant students toe the line: threat of examinations. You may skip my classes, ignore my homework, sell the textbook, and burn my notes, but I am waiting for you on the day of reckoning, and we shall see then who has the last laugh. Here is the question paper. Ten questions. Answer any seven. You will have a tough time deciding which seven, and a tougher time trying to answer them. Write to the point. All the rough work has to be written on the paper. Marks will be deducted for unclear handwriting. Correction will be stiff. And there is a sharp watch in the examination hall for cribbing or copying. Any infraction of the rules will be severely dealt with. See you there.

Manipulation. For their own good, of course, as manipulation by well-meaning people aways is, but plain and naked manipulation nonetheless. I have the rod in my hand and can wield it efficiently to make knees bend into submission and minds into acquiescence. It will no longer be love of mathematics or need of a degree or desire to learn that will bring the student to his desk and to his books in the night hours of repeated vigils, but fear of the examination. Right behavior and wrong motivation. Whatever benefits the knowledge of mathematics brings to the young person's life, the harm caused by the presence of fear in his wavering mind will offset them all. We impart knowledge and we cripple souls. We call that education.

Once I went to meet my classes, chalk and eraser in hand, at ten forty-five in the morning in the usual classroom. I stood at the door of the classroom exactly thirty seconds before the bell, with the ruthless punctuality I took pride in, and waited. Then I noticed something strange. The classroom was empty. Had I mistaken the place or the time? I checked the timetable. This was the classroom, and this was the hour. And not a student in sight. Never before had such a thing happened to me. Was there any strike? No. I looked around, and a fellow lecturer in a similar plight came close and explained the situation. A famous movie star (matinee idol, according to the local press) was visiting the university campus that morning for a charity function. The place was nearby, the students were well informed, and for once had decided unanimously to forgo learning, which could always be postponed, in favor of the unique opportunity to get a glimpse of greatness. And off they went, all of them, girls and boys, leaving their teacher in a lonely corridor with chalk and eraser in hand to muse on the relative values of the young and the old. I waited the statutory five minutes, and withdrew to plan my vengeance.

Next day the class was full. Total silence on the benches. I affected indifference and said, "The theorems and problems that were to have been done yesterday are found on such and such pages in the textbook. They will not be explained in class, though they will form part of the matter for the coming examination. We now proceed to the next lesson." And so we did. The time for the examination came, and I watched the papers carefully. The question they all had answered best was the one taken from the untaught lesson. They all were sure that portion would be asked, and they had prepared it with special care. I came to the conclusion that if more movie stars would grace our campus with their presence, my students would learn more mathematics—and hate it more.

There is a dreadful word in our daily vocabulary today: *terrorism*. The reign of terror, the tyranny of intimidation, the multinational of fear. Pressure and extortion and injustice and crime made possible on an international scale because we all are afraid. The dismal trade of oppression and blood runs and thrives literally on fear. Free the prisoners or we'll blow up the plane; pay the ransom or we'll kill the hostages. And we pay the money and free the criminals because we are afraid of death, afraid of criticism, afraid of political repercussions, afraid of blackmail. We all complain of the scourge of terrorism in our days, and we all cooperate with it by holding on to life and being afraid to lose it. We are vulnerable because we are afraid, and fanatic people take advantage of our weakness to further their causes.

But they too are afraid. Terror extends its reign to the heart of the dealers in terror. Terrorists have been known to kill those of their ranks who had left them to integrate themselves back into law-abiding society. They are afraid that their numbers will dwindle if defections are allowed, and so they kill their own companions when they leave their terrorist activities and return to a peaceful life. They must feel terribly insecure when they see doubts in the members of their own organization and even in their own hearts. If people begin to leave us, where do we stand? If members of the group desert, what happens to the group? How then to prevent them from leaving? Frighten them. Use against them the weapon so effectively used by them against others. The weapon of terror. Kill those who leave the group so that nobody will dare to leave after them. Fear of death will make them stay, as it makes others pay ransom money or yield to any demands. Terror is dealt out to the dealers in terror. The blackmailers are blackmailed. He who lives by the sword will die by the sword. The reign of fear is consummated. It was Robert Frost who said, "There is nothing I'm afraid of like scared people." Terrorists are scared; and they scare all of us into the most abject submission history has seen. The terrorists' demands are eventually met, and mankind is the weaker for it.

I dream of the day when the crew and passengers who board a commercial airliner in a regular flight will sign a voluntary pledge that in the event of their plane being commandeered by terrorists, they will not accept any rescue nor yield to any demands, but freely choose to offer the sacrifice of their lives for the peace of the world. Such a stand, heroic no doubt and unheard-of for a start, would eventually put an end to all hijackings, as the hijackers are intelligent enough to realize that they gain nothing by ending up each time with a massacre on their hands and no concessions. They might put to the test once or twice such brave pledges, but would soon give up, and indeed this might be the only way to end the plague of threats, blackmail, hijackings, and kidnappings that sadly characterize the age of air travel and deadly explosives.

I say this to bring to the clearest possible light the fact that it is our fear that lays us open to manipulation. Fear is the handle we ourselves give to those who would turn us around at their will. Terrorism exists because we are afraid. There are international commissions that meet regularly to analyze the spread of terrorism and propose remedies. They are not likely to do away with the plague. The ultimate remedy lies in the human heart. Fearlessness alone can free us from the snares our own fears have built.

I know I am dreaming, but someone else dreamt the same dream much before, and put it into practice. Jesus let violence have its way with him, rather than resisting with twelve legions of angels, to show us the way to end all violence. If someone is ready to face death, there is nothing that can bend his will or frighten him into subservience. Readiness to die is the secret to living. Faith is the end of fear.

THE FEAR OF GOD

Scholars tell us that the word *religion* is used in only two passages in the whole Bible. (For the curious soul, these are Acts 26:5 and James 1:26–27.) The normal biblical expression to refer to what we call religion is *fear of God*. In the pages of the Old and New testaments, to fear God means to honor him as God, to revere him and worship him with the supreme adoration that is due to him alone. The followers of the true God are those "who fear the Lord," and God loves and rewards those "who fear him." Even in heaven the elect fear God, according to the Book of Revelation (15:4), and this clearly shows that such a fear is not any obsequious submission or servile trepidation, but the essential attitude of created man before the transcendent majesty of the Creator. "The fear of the Lord is glory and honor, is joy and crown of exultation. The fear of God gladdens the heart, brings pleasure and delight. He who fears the Lord will come to a good end; the Lord will bless him at the hour of his death. The fear of the Lord is the beginning of wisdom" (Sirach 1:11–14).

This is undoubtedly true, and the feeling of awe and wonder that fills a person in the presence of his Maker is an intrinsic dimension of the religious experience on earth. However, it is also true that once the concept of religious fear comes into the hands of a human, it is liable to be misunderstood and misused, and may even lead to the complexes and deviations associated with human fear in general. The meaningful and beneficent concept of religious fear may degenerate in practice into scruples, doubts, and intimidation that are far from the original intent but all too real given our capacity to turn a genuine help into harmful hindrance.

The danger comes when religious fear is used, with better or worse intention, to manipulate unguarded believers into blind submission. The temptation to abuse power is never far from those who wield it, and religious power in people's consciences is greater than any military or political power. Do this or God will punish you. Forbidding words which no mortal should dare to pronounce of himself, and which, nevertheless, in literal expression or in equivalent intention are not so rarely heard in religious dealings among serious people. Out of reverence for the name of God and out of respect for those who in one way or another represent him, devout people will readily accept the verdict and feel guilty if they do not conform to the established norm. Consciences are very delicate ground, and the utmost delicacy is required to enter them. Manipulation of consciences is the worst manipulation.

I was once staying in a very poor village in India when I learned that two monks from a well-known religious sect had come to the village in their yearly round to collect funds for their institutions. The people were poor, and the village small, so I felt the monks would have to depart almost empty-handed, and I said so. The villagers were very kindhearted and would surely make an effort to give some satisfaction to two people whom they considered ministers of God, but there was an obvious limit to their generosity, and the total amount could not come to much. When I spoke to that effect, the people simply kept quiet. The two monks stayed overnight and departed late on the following day. After they had gone, people mentioned the sum of money they had taken with them from the village. I could not believe it. It amounted to the earnings of the whole village for one month. The people had no savings, no cash, and even if they wanted, they could not have collected that money in that time. True, there were moneylenders in nearby villages, but their terms were brutally abusive and they were only a desperate last resource in case of a real personal or family need. This was only a religious tribute by monks who showed themselves in the village at this time of the year and for this purpose. Yet the information was true. The sum had been given. How had it happened?

The monks had named the sum they expected, and had added that if it was not delivered in cash the next day, they would curse the village in the name of God. That did it. The villagers humbly acknowledged their defeat. The people were poor, but were afraid of the curse. They would do anything not to incur the holy men's displeasure. They gathered the money and gave it promptly. God knows what sacrifices every family would have to bear for months to come because of that unholy tribute. But religious fear was greater than fear of want. A whole village had been manipulated into misery in the name of God. The monks were given an honorable send-off, and they continued undaunted their begging trip according to plan. They would not fail to reach the amount they had fixed.

This external example is again image and parable of the more subtle manipulations we submit ourselves to, where it is not money that is surrendered but ideas and principles and behavior. We manipulate ourselves and each other into doing things out of fear, we suppress our own freedom and act against our best judgment for the sake of safety. In my heart of hearts I believe a certain action is not necessary, yet I indefectibly perform it, not only out of fear of society and adverse criticism if I do not conform to its norms, but out of my own inner insecurity, which recoils from taking the risk of being different and ignoring a rule all others follow. I honestly do not think such a behavior of mine pleases God. He would appreciate more honest dissent in me than servile submission. With sensitivity not to shock people or harm anyone, with responsibility and seriousness, I can reason my stand and choose my path. God will love me to be free with him. It is I, in my fear and lack of faith, who do not dare to be free with him. And the forced behavior continues. I do not see in it my own good, and I do not see in it God's glory.

The Gandhian thinker Kakasaheb Kalelkar cites an example from his own experience with his usual depth and wit. For a time during his work in Maharashtra he had to share living quarters with an engineer from Poona called Lele. This Mr. Lele was a Saraswat Brahman, as was Kalelkar, but he soon made it clear in his daily conversations that he was an atheist, and did not in any way believe in God. Still, Kalelkar noticed that the atheistic engineer said his morning and night prayers without fail, following all the Brahmanic rubrics of the *Gayatri Mantra* and the *Sandhya*, which not even Kalelkar himself observed so carefully. Finally his curiosity got the better of him, and he said to his roommate, "You say that you don't believe in God, yet I see you every day, morning and evening, at your prayers with unfailing regularity. I don't want to intrude in your privacy, but if I can ask, can you explain to me that contradiction?" "Oh yes," said the atheistic Brahman engineer. "In fact, it is quite simple. It is a fact that I do not believe in God. I am personally convinced that there is no such thing as God. Yet . . . just in case . . . I want to be on the safe side, and if in the end it turns out that there is a God, I want to have a clear account with him, and so I pay him my daily respects morning and evening as a good Brahman. Sensible after all, isn't it?"

Quite sensible. In fact, too sensible, in my opinion. The good Brahman went too far in his desire for safety. I honestly do not think God approves of that kind of worship. He does not enjoy bringing people to their knees in spite of themselves out of fear and trembling. If you believe, do kneel down and worship with the sincerity of your heart in the prayer of your lips; but if you do not believe, stay where you are and be content with your thought. An honest atheist is better than a fake believer. Paul, in Romans, states the principle that God will judge by the Law those who have the Law (Jews), and without the Law those who do not have the Law (Gentiles), which is a very clear way of saying that God will judge each one according to his sincere convictions. The person's conscience is what ultimately matters. God sees the heart and cannot be cheated by the flawless performance of external rubrics. And to think that he would be sardonically pleased by watching a man cowering down to reluctant prayer out of sheer fear is, I believe, unworthy of God. He is not a God of compulsion but of freedom.

When I first came upon that story, I used it triumphantly to show up the weakness of atheism and the precarious condition of its followers. I gloated over the lack of consistency in the engineer's behavior, and his implicit recognition of God in the midst of his repeated denial. In other words, I was using the story to instill fear into persons with religious doubts to make sure they would stay within the fold. I was playing on their feelings of insecurity to guarantee their perseverance. That was well meant, but in doing so, I was guilty of the same fallacy as

the safety-conscious Brahman; I was using fear to force
compliance. I had missed the real message, which I now
see. The deeper point of the story is not how to force an
atheist to pray against his own conviction, but rather how
to liberate the mind from fears that lead us to cheat
ourselves and to try to cheat God. The lesson is not "Even
if you do not believe in God, pray to him," but rather, "If
you do not believe in God, do not pray to him." Luther
said that the first rule in prayer is honesty to God, and we
cannot please him by faking feelings or pretending belief.
God is more honored by our sincerity than by our flattery.

If we truly have a genuine conviction, let us have the
courage to live up to it. Atheism is an extreme case, of
course, and I take the story again only as a parable to
illustrate a point; but in smaller matters and lesser attitudes
we may find, if we carefully look into our lives, that we too
are bowing down to a custom, a rubric, a rule without
genuine conviction, only to make sure—just in case!—as
the wary Brahman did. Such behavior does not do us
honor and, in the long run, does not foster the true
interests of religion.

That in the Bible fear of the Lord has a positive meaning
and is practically equivalent to love of the Lord is clear
from its texts. The one effective rule of Hebrew poetry is
parallelism, by which the same idea appears in consecutive
verses with different words and one meaning. The parallel
expressions create a rhythm that drives home the single
meaning. This is the strength of the following verses from
Sirach 2:15–16:

> Those who fear the Lord obey his words;
> those who love him follow his ways.
> Those who fear the Lord strive to please him;
> those who love him fulfil his law.

In those clear verses, as in the whole mentality that inspired them, love and fear are interchangeable expressions that complement each other by underlining different aspects of our relationship to the one supreme reality that is God. God is Father, and so we love him as children, but God is also Lord, and the reverential fear that his majesty inspires tempers our familiarity and enhances our reverence. Fear signifies the transcendence of God, as love denotes his proximity to us. In that healthy and balanced sense the fear of the Lord is truly the beginning of wisdom.

SIXTEEN POSTCARDS

Here are a few simple examples from my observation in which it seems to me that the element of fear in religion has been overstressed while the element of love was played down, with the result that God appears more as a tyrant to be feared than a friend to be trusted. This distortion is important because our life is what our concept of God is; and our relationship with him, which derives from that concept, is what marks our behavior and directs our course. If that relationship is based on love and trust, we shall flower as persons, live in joy, and die in peace; but if our relationship with God is one of suspicion and fear, we shall cringe and shrivel in our souls, and our minds will be an easy prey to all the evils that insecurity can bring.

I lived once for one full year with a parish priest who told me the trial God had sent him shortly before I went to stay with him. He was a very methodical and faithful worker who fulfilled all his duties with meticulous care. But the previous year, so he explained to me, he had dropped the public procession on the day of Corpus Christi simply because he felt too lazy to organize it. He had held the procession regularly for all the many years he had been in charge of the parish, though that took a good deal of preparation and labor. He had to coax the people to come, prepare the dresses and images, rehearse with each one what he or she had to do, buy sweets to give to the children after the function (he commented realistically that it was the sweets that made the procession), and preside then himself at the long ceremony in the sweltering heat. He had done it faithfully every year, but just for once that year he had felt lazy, had kept quiet, and there had been no sweets and no procession. Nobody protested: in fact, nobody seemed to have noticed the omission, and the date passed without the festivities.

Shortly after the nonevent, however, a calamity overtook the parish. The church was looted, the tabernacle broken open, the sacred vessels stolen, and the Eucharist desecrated. There was consternation in all the faithful, and guilt in the priest's conscience. He said publicly, "God has punished me. I failed in my duty, suppressing the procession this year on my own, and so God has sent us a calamity more dreadful than we had ever encountered in our parish, the profanation of our church. The fault is mine. I accept the divine punishment, and I promise before all that I will never again omit the solemn procession. Pray that God may forgive me."

He was much older and wiser than I was, yet I tried to put before him another way of looking at what had happened. I could not imagine that God, who knew well the long, faithful service of his minister, had been watching for his first slip, and as soon as the first negligence came, thundered from heaven and decided to have the church looted to distress and humiliate the guilty priest. Such an image of God is unjust, cruel, and offensive, a projection of man's own fears and meanness into an anthropomorphized God. We only know that there have been two events, the dropping of the procession and the looting of the church, but we have no right to establish a relationship between the two and say that the first caused the second. Only God knows about that, and his counsel is unfathomable. There may conceivably be other parishes where a procession has been omitted and the church has not been looted. And would God choose such a mortifying and irreligious way to punish a humble priest? I tried all my arguments in order to console the good priest, but nothing I could say would change his reasoning or lessen his grief. He had sinned and he had been punished. He would never omit the procession again. At least the children could get their sweets.

Several times in my life, both in readings and in actual situations, I have encountered an attitude that is praiseworthy at first sight, but in my opinion, hides a wrong concept of God and his justice. A mother prays to God that he may take the sickness away from her child and give it to her, who will willingly suffer it to save her child. The same may happen between friends or, in a well-known Indian legend, between a loyal subject and his king. Someone falls sick, and someone else, who loves him, prays that his friend may be saved and he may suffer instead. Real cases in which such prayer has been made and heard are then reported from mouth to mouth, and a sense of awe overcomes all those who hear the story and bow before God's designs. Here is an actual case from an outstanding person I knew well, and who told it with winning simplicity and great feeling in his autobiography. Gurudayal Mallikji worked first under Rabindranath Tagore and then under Mahatma Gandhi, enjoying always their full confidence, and in their name and with their inspiration and guidance he organized the voluntary service to aid the Indian refugees from Pakistan after the partition of the two nations. He was a perpetually cheerful personality, and wore a distinctive white beard; his dialogues combined the wisdom of the prophet with the wit of the humorist. He underwent a deep experience in his youth, and this is how he told it to Mukulbhai Kalarthi in his spoken autobiography.

Those were the days of the plague of Quetta, a black memory of medieval horror in our own century in the lives of people who are still alive today. The unnamed sickness spread with deadly swiftness across the northern plains, taking in village after village under the pallor of its silent death. Nobody could tell who would fall and who would escape. Death had no preferences. Young and old, men and women, strong and weak, could be struck alike or be spared alike. Under the same roof three died and one was saved, or all died or all were saved, but the mortal uncertainty hung on all homes with equal terror for days on end. Suddenly a person would break into acid sweat, black tumors would appear under the armpits, and within hours he would breathe his last. No medicine helped. People died quietly, resignedly, silently, and the problem in the villages was not how to save the living but how to cremate the dead. In those nightmarish conditions, Mallikji recalls, an aunt of his went down with the plague. The family gathered round her, and her sister, that is, Mallikji's mother, made at that moment this simple spontaneous prayer, and all heard it: "Lord, my sister has two very small children, and if she dies, the children will suffer without their mother. I too have children, but they are big and do not need me. Save my sister and take my life instead. I give it willingly." That was exactly what happened. The aunt improved, the ominous symptoms disappeared, and she was soon out of all danger. Simultaneously Mallikji's mother developed the symptoms, sank, and died. Her prayer had been heard and her sacrifice accepted. His mother's death in such a selfless manner impressed Mallikji so deeply that he resolved to consecrate his life to the service of others, and to do that more freely and effectively, he never married and led a truly generous and dedicated life into ripe old age. His mother's memory was his constant inspiration throughout his holy life.

These are sacred grounds, and the utmost reverence is called for while trying to understand what is going on here. There is deep faith, selfless love, lofty sacrifice, and a noble heritage of the best sentiments mankind has known. Together with that, however, there is a concept of God that does not correspond to those refined feelings, and it rather jars with such a privileged background. God appears here as an insensitive tyrant who is only concerned with getting his victim for the day, whoever he or she may be. A human life has to be offered; never mind whose it is, provided one person dies. Almost like Nazi authorities in concentration camps when they accepted voluntary swapping of death victims, provided the number was kept. If God had really heard the touching prayer of that heroic mother, could he not have saved the two sisters to reward their generosity and make a whole family rejoice with the blessing of his power? God's judgment, of course, is known only to himself, and he can draw long-range benefits from present calamities; far from us to impose on him our shortsighted criteria. But what does fall under our purview is man's attitude toward God, and in this respect, the untutored image that emerges from this incident is that of a God who cares only for his pound of flesh no matter where it comes from. Pay my tribute, and the account is closed. As a rather anticlerical Hindu saying goes regarding marriage fees, "Let the bride perish, let the bridegroom perish, but let the officiating priest have his fee." I do not in any way pretend to judge God's actions, and I most deeply respect the delicate feelings of all the people involved in this episode, while I feel honored by my personal acquaintance with Mallikji and I

am willing witness to the ennobling effect such an inher-
itance had for him. But at the same time I unequivocally
reject a concept of God that reduces him to a retribution
machine. It is a rather popular concept, and it is danger-
ously erroneous.

I have kept with me as a specimen one of the several
postcards I have received, all part of the same game some
religious-minded people play at regular intervals. The
card is unsigned and says, "You are to write sixteen
postcards like this, with the name of the 'Easy-to-Please
Mother' on them, and ask each of the recipients to write
sixteen similar cards. If you fail to do so, some great
calamity will overtake you. People have been known to
die for breaking this holy chain. To the glory of the
Easy-to-Please Mother!" The Easy-to-Please Mother (San-
toshi Mata) is a popular goddess in India whose reassuring
name does not seem to have been understood by some of
her fervent devotees. They threaten with dire calamities
anyone who may dare to break the chain of postcards,
which at the rate of sixteen to one would soon be flooding
every post office in the country if some doughty souls
would not come forward to brave the curse and save the
mail. I have consistently broken all such chains, whenever
any hidden acquaintance has tried to make me a link in
any of them, and I am still hale and hearty. What I cannot
avoid is a feeling of annoyance when I get such postcards.
Whom do they take me for? If they trust my compliance,
why do they add the threats? And if they suspect my
noncooperation, what makes them think they can force
me to a reluctant worship? And how can they appreciate
such a reluctant worship? What value can a postcard
written out of fear have in their minds? How can they
imagine a goddess is honored by a heap of shabby,
anonymous, unwilling postcards? They know themselves

to have been the victims of this ignoble game because someone knew their address and passed the baby on to them, and all they want to see is how to pass the baby on to someone else, with the added grievance of the multiplying coefficient. Like the holy man's ashes, they pass from hand to hand till someone has the courage to throw them into the dustbin. The ambitious scheme always breaks down. It is consoling to realize that all such chains break eventually. The sooner the better.

All these cases bring out the human limitation in understanding divine ideas. Our finite intellect can never exhaust the infinitude of God. The danger is that in choosing traits of the divinity, our own complexes may lead us to overstress the less amiable ones as a projection of our own fears. We fear the worst, and seek protection from our own terrors in extreme practices. Our need for safety overrides our best judgment and makes us conceive outlandish notions with dangerous ease. A god that trades victims is at best a pagan god, a Baal or Moloch that has to be appeased by a daily offering in blind submission. That concept does no honor to God nor to us. If we call God Father, let us at least give him the credit to act as a Father, not as a cruel tyrant in thoughtless retribution. To me the puzzle is how people who attribute such a behavior to God can still relate to him and pray and worship. I guess the explanation is that fear has them in its grip, and so they are afraid to discontinue religious practices even when to them they have no more meaning.

H. G. Wells describes a pious woman with the phrase "With her to believe was to fear" (*In the Days of the Comet*). That is not the biblical fear anymore, full of reverence, respect, and love, but a servile fear that degrades faith to superstition and religion to anxiety. Such harsh concepts may secretly estrange us from prayer and worship and we may find ourselves drying up in our devotion or wavering in our faith. The concept of God is our most precious possession, and anything that tarnishes it enfeebles our life.

The people of Israel had projected onto God their fears to such an extent that they were afraid to approach him. We live in a new and different age, the age of God-with-us, and have the privilege and the joy to let that holy intimacy flourish in our lives in humble simplicity and daily gratitude. Let us be "the children of the promise" as we are meant to be.

THE SNARES OF SECURITY

When I point out the role insecurity plays in weakening our stand and shaking our lives, as I have been doing from the first chapter of this book, I may give the impression that insecurity is something to be done away with, and the less of it we have, the better. Insecurity appears as the cause of much harm done to us, and therefore as something to be fought, defeated, conquered, so that we achieve a state of internal security, and with it balance, health, and peace. This impression is wrong and it is time to correct it and gain truer perspectives. It is not possible to do away with insecurity, and even if it were possible, it is not desirable. The point is not that we are to suppress insecurity but to learn how to live with it; not to ban it but to harness it to our best interests in the working of our minds and the living of our lives.

In fact, it is security that is dangerous and harmful. Shakespeare said, "For ye all know: security is mortal's chiefest enemy." Security is our enemy because it lures us into complacency, favors the status quo, and encourages laziness. All is well, nothing is to be feared, everything is safe, and we have nothing to worry about. This is the sort of declaration our lazy mind is longing to hear. Relax, take it easy, no more efforts to be made, no more summits to be conquered. Lower your defenses and cancel your plans. We have labored enough, and now we have only to reap the fruit of our labors. Perfect setting for a moral collapse.

I have painfully lived a long experience that exemplifies the enervating role of security in our work, and at the same time throws light on the ways and institutions of our modern welfare states. When I joined the teaching staff of the college that has been my academic home through my professional life, appointments were given on merit, and could be terminated by the principal without more ado if the teacher failed to give satisfaction. Complaints by the students, inquiry, warnings, probation, further complaints, three-month notice, and a vacancy in the staff. Everybody knew that, and so everybody was on his best behavior, classes were prepared, discipline kept, punctuality observed, and high standards maintained with general satisfaction. Several elements combine to bring out the best in a good teacher: an academic atmosphere, proper recognition, keenness in the students, challenging questions, inner vocation, personal gifts, communication skills; but with all that, the persisting realization that one's job depends on one's performance is indispensable motivation for consistent effort. Today that motivation is no longer there. A teacher's tenure is absolutely safe from the day of his appointment, and no principal with all his power and no students with all their complaints can ever remove a teacher, however ineffective his teaching may have become. There are rules and unions and boycotts and pressures, and the teacher's security has to be safeguarded above all. It is. And the quality of the teaching is the worse for it. Security has brought indifference, negligence, and stagnation. There are other reasons, to be sure, but job security has played a fundamental part in the lowering of academic standards among us.

This very example can help to fix more exactly the balance between security and insecurity that can best suit our development and our work. Total security freezes progress, but total insecurity can also create such tensions that the mind ceases working and no further development is possible. Sociology and economics will debate the advantages and disadvantages of competition versus protectionism; meanwhile psychology takes the situation as it is and sees how the person and the group can best advance in the existing circumstances. Let the insecurity remain, and let the person develop inner strength to cope with the insecurity and respond to the danger of dismissal not with immobilizing panic but with the controlled display of his best qualities and greatest strength. The danger is a challenge, and challenge is the climate for man to shake his innate laziness and give of his best in the face of difficulties. Let me feel my own insecurity, not in order to despair and run away, but in order to wake up and raise my own strength and join battle and claim victory. Yes, I know that my students are not interested in mathematics, that the impossible syllabus expects every student to be an incarnation of Einstein, which none of them is, that all they care for is to pass the exam by hook or by crook, while all the principal wants is discipline in class, silence in the corridors, and high grades in the final result. I'll show them now. I know my stuff, I know how to put it across, I know how to handle the students and motivate them for their own good, and I welcome this opportunity to pull out all my stops and show what I can do. It is not going to be a dull job in any case!

Insecurity remains, but it is now an ally, an incentive, a spring that propels us into action. Thus we learn to value its positive effects and we even come to enjoy the thrill of adventure and the taste of danger. All growth entails risk, and the risks of insecurity can enliven the process of living. A game is no fun if the result is fixed before it starts. To enjoy the game of life, we must open ourselves to the vicissitudes it brings us day by day. The best way to tame insecurity is to welcome it wholeheartedly. It is the spice of life.

Alan Watts goes even further. He writes, "Insecurity is the result of trying to be secure," and confirms the paradoxical thesis with a quick appeal to common and divine sense: "When you try to stay on the surface of the water, you sink; but when you try to sink you float. When you hold your breath you lose it—which immediately calls to mind an ancient and much neglected saying, 'Whosoever would save his soul shall lose it.' "* If I try to hold the reins tight, I become tense and make the horses restive under the pull of the bit in their mouths and my impatience in their ears. The more I want to control them, the stiffer I become and the greater fear I feel that they may go wild and throw me down a cliff, and my fear communicates to them and makes the situation increasingly dangerous. If I trust my horses and let them use their wisdom and show their loyalty, they will not throw themselves, and me with them, down any precipice but will safely reach, and make me reach with them, the final destination.

If I want to make sure that the accounts are correct, I set another man to check the work of the first. But if I do not trust the first man, how can I trust the second? In fact, my fear has already manifested itself in the fact that I have appointed a second man to check the first, and now logic demands I have a third man check on the second. Suspicion increases. I am worse now than when I started. No report by any accountant will satisfy me. Total security is impossible. And if from money matters I pass to the much more subtle and important and impossible-to-check

* Alan W. Watts, *The Wisdom of Insecurity* (New York: Vintage Books, 1968), 9.

business of the soul and its principles and beliefs and actions and behavior, I find that security evades me, and the more I want to make sure, the less sure I feel, and my search for guarantees turns out to be an exposure of my weaknesses. My longing for security only serves to uncover my insecurity and intensify it by trying to run away from it. Whatever efforts I make, I shall never obtain full security, and anything short of full security is no security, so that my very efforts underline my failure and I feel more insecure at the end than at the beginning.

To me this is the deeper meaning and value of faith in our life. Faith is in practice the capacity to live in a world of doubt under a promise of truth. Faith does not do away with our human condition, our limited vision, our wavering mind, but it does give us the power to walk where the earth is not firm, to see where the air is not clear, to set sail when the sea is not calm; the power to hope in the midst of despondency, to love in the midst of indifference, to smile in the midst of misunderstanding. We remain very much in the world with our finitude, our limitations, our insecurity; but we have a glimpse of the truth that is clear and firm and eternal, and with that gentle ray of light we direct our steps through the surrounding darkness. Faith is not an insurance policy but a courageous adventure, not a tranquilizer but a challenge, not a bed of roses but a battlefront. Faith does not take away the veil of mystery but teaches us to look through it in wonder and hope. The true understanding of faith prepares the mind for the risks of life on earth under God's loving gaze.

I knew a priest who went to confession every day without fail throughout the whole year to the end of his life. What took him daily to the confessional was not, by his own explanation, need or scruple, but the desire not to die without having received the sacrament of reconciliation in the last twenty-four hours of his life. He wanted a fresh forgiveness of sin just before departure. An understandable wish, but not without inconveniences. Apart from the considerable exertion to which he must have submitted his ingenuity in order to find some suitable self-accusation every twenty-four hours, and the trouble he must have put the obliging confessor to, and without underestimating in any way his undoubted piety and his practical appreciation of the sacrament, I sensed a latent misunderstanding in his persevering observance. He wanted to make sure, he wanted to take no chances, he wanted to force God's hand to win admission into heaven under any circumstances; he left nothing to God's mercy and wanted to arrive at the gates of heaven with all the certificates duly signed and stamped to force his way into the heavenly mansions. I may have sinned, but here is the official pardon with today's date on it. Open the gates and show me to my seat. I have full right to it, as all my papers are in order.

I exaggerate for clarity, but that, to my reading, was the direction along which that spiritually perfectionist mind was moving. And the direction is initially misleading and ultimately wrong. Confession is not meant to give us security by giving us official clearance; rather the contrary: by going to confession, we show our need to be pardoned, a need that will always continue to the end of our days, and we leave our future in God's hands with full trust in his loving mercy. Our salvation lies, not in demonstrating our innocence, but in acknowledging our unworthiness. In our terminology here, our safety lies, not in achieving security, but in accepting insecurity. That is the core of faith.

THE URGE TO MAXIMIZE PLEASURE

To learn how to live with insecurity means to accept the fact that insecurity is to stay with us for life, to observe its action on us, and once we know it, to neutralize the bad effects we may have discovered. Here are some of these bad effects for awareness and correction.

Insecurity leads us to try to maximize pleasure, and this tendency to maximize pleasure works eventually against itself and destroys the very pleasure it seeks. If I do not obtain the maximum pleasure, I feel frustrated; and if I obtain it, I feel surfeited. I feel an appetite, I eat beyond my needs, I feel bloated, I abhor the very sight of food. Or I do not get enough food for my appetite, and then I feel hungry and threatened. The need for total pleasure deprives me of possible pleasure. I always need to get the highest enjoyment, have the best time, get the most out of every entertainment. I am not satisfied with a second-rate show, I feel the best is due me, and consider myself cheated if it is not given to me at once. I am the first to realize that this inordinate craving for pleasure defeats its own purpose, and I would like to control it and keep it within bounds. And so the first thing I want to do is understand where the craving comes from.

It comes from my insecurity. I know pleasure is hard to come by, I am not sure when I shall have another occasion for it, and consequently I feel an inner compulsion to make the best of the present chance up to its upmost limits. If I were reassured, not only in my conscious mind, which intellectually knows it, but in my subconscious, which instinctively fears the opposite, that good days will come again and chances for joy will not be missing in the future, I could relax and go easy about the present chance and enjoy it without seeking to exhaust it as if all the pleasure I were ever to get in life were to come from this one occasion. If I felt secure, I could plan my days and space out my pleasures and wait for their time and enjoy the small satisfactions as pledges of greater future ones without trying to blow up each small enjoyment into a historic celebration. But I feel insecure and so I grab at each instant of pleasure as though it were the only one I would ever be able to enjoy, and in the process I spoil the genuine pleasure I could have obtained, had I been at peace.

We have inherited this unfortunate instinct from our remote ancestors. Primitive peoples led a precarious existence and were never sure where their next meal would come from. In such circumstances it was understandable that they would eat each time as much as they could, just in case the next meal would be late in coming, so that they would not go hungry. It was an existential need to make the best of every meal, and similarly of every pleasure, as life was uncertain and living conditions hard. Their radical insecurity made them instinctively possessive of food and pleasure with the quick intensity of instant satisfaction. No trusting the future. Eat today the hunted game against the days of want that may follow.

We are safe in the matter of food, our meals are secure,

we know for sure that at the next mealtime there will be a table laid and warm food on it for our regular refection. Yet the ancestral instinct is inscribed on our genes and it prompts us to eat beyond our need as though there would be no next meal for an indefinite length of time. Outwardly we eat with spoons and forks out of china dishes with impeccable table manners, but inwardly the jungle savage is hurriedly gobbling chunks of raw meat to loading capacity as insurance against the lean days he foresees ahead. Irrational craving for food in an overfed society.

When I was reading for my mathematics degree at Madras University, there was on the premises a large cage with an enormous python, the outlandish pet of a stout-hearted professor of English. It was harmless enough, and I submitted to the foolhardy ritual of having myself photographed with the python around my neck, thick as it was like a truck tire, heavy as a sack of stones, and hard as iron. A poster by the cage invited the students, "Bring a bandicoot." That was food for the snake. The supply was irregular. One day several students would bring their outsized rodents, and the python would devour them all without a second thought, and then a few days may follow without a bandicoot. The python followed the jungle law: Eat when you have and wait while you have not. The difference between the python and us was that after a multiple feast, it rejected food for several days, even if offered to it. Its warden knew its habits and would say, "Not inclined. Come tomorrow." And the snake continued its fast undisturbed. We, on the contrary, even if we have eaten more than our fill, when the time for the next meal comes, go again obediently to the dining room and eat our meal even without an appetite. We obey the clock, not the stomach; we unhappily combine the readiness of primitive man to eat each time as much as possible with the regularity of modern man to eat at fixed times in daily routine. Our bodies are the worse for it.

Food is only one example. The same tendency to maximize pleasure because we are not sure when we shall have it again applies to all our activities, even in the more spiritual areas like friendship and love. Every meeting between friends has to be a success, every party enjoyed with frenzy, every conversation treasured with delight, or at once both parties will fear there is something wrong with their friendship. The very insecurity in their mutual affection and dependence compels them to try to make every meeting memorable and to reassure one another at the end, "It was great, wasn't it?" If the two friends are secure in their love, they will not need to work themselves up to a summit of emotion each time, they will tolerate silences and bear with dullness, they will be able to combine permanent nearness with temporary estrangements in the delicate interplay of close intimacy. Insecurity always tends to grab whatever comes to hand for fear of losing it. When we want to learn how to cope with the insecurity that will always accompany us through our earthly journey, one of the detrimental effects we have to guard ourselves against is this compulsion to hold on to things, to possess objects and persons, to maximize pleasure out of the fear of losing it. To remove this compulsion is to remove the sting of insecurity.

This is nothing else than the paradox of love: I love you and I leave you free. First I feel that I cannot live without you, and so in the name of my love I want to grab you, to hold you, to make sure that you will never leave me, will always be close to me. But when doing that, I realize that I am ruining our love, and that trying to make sure of holding you is the best way to lose you. And so in the risk that is love, in supreme trust and sublime sacrifice, I leave you entirely free to remain or to go, to speak or to be silent, to look at me or to forget me. That is the ultimate insecurity, and in that insecurity, known and accepted, dreaded and enjoyed, is the test, the worth, the flowering of love in all its beauty and strength. I cannot be without you, and therefore I have to let you be you, that is, to be free in the hope and the risk that in your freedom you will find yourself and my love in you, and you will stay with me of your own free will and in your genuine pleasure. To let go is the paradoxical way, and the only true way, to possess in love.

Another aspect of the same pull of insecurity toward compulsive pleasure and secure possession is the desire to protect ourselves by convincing ourselves that our position is the best in the sense that the group we belong to, the ideas we hold, and the customs we follow are the best. The cover of the "best" to eliminate the temptation to follow the lesser gods. "We look for security by fortifying and enclosing ourselves in innumerable ways. We want the protection of being 'exclusive' and 'special,' seeking to belong to the safest church, the best nation, the highest class, the right set, and the 'nice' people. These defenses lead to divisions between us, and so to more insecurity demanding more defenses. Of course it is all done in the sincere belief that we are trying to do the right things and live in the best way."* The compulsion for the best is part of the tendency to ensure safety. I want to be sure that what I am doing is the best so that I need not worry about comparisons or criticisms. I am safe in the loftiness of my incontestable choice.

I still suffer when I have to choose among many others

* Alan W. Watts, *The Wisdom of Insecurity* (New York: Vintage Books, 1968), 78.

one book to read or one record to play, because I want to make sure that the book is the best available to me now, and so is the music in the record. I want the best for me, not because of personal conceit but as part of my need to maximize pleasure and to build around me a defense of impregnable excellence. I do not realize that by trying to increase my security, I am only laying myself open to greater insecurity. By taking refuge in the best, I am perpetually challenged by the second best. Would not the other book have been better? Was not Bruckner more fitting for my mood now than Brahms? No end of it. The true attitude that leads to peace is to choose what reasonably appeals to me at the moment, knowing full well that other occupations and other ideas and other authors are equally acceptable, and that there will be options open for them at their time. I am not going to be listening to Mozart all the time.

A WALKING STICK

Insecurity leads us to find refuge in others. The group, the crowd, the institution. The individual cannot survive on his own, and therefore seeks the support of others. Who can afford to be original in his thinking, free in his principles, independent in his behavior? Very few men and women, and at a very high risk. The majority follow the pattern set out for them by the society they were born in, and find in it the safety of knowing they are doing what all are doing and thinking what all are thinking. This process begins in childhood and lasts until old age, and is sharpest at the two extremes. In between, its ups and downs shape the personality of the subject in his bouts of independence and his periods of subservience. A person is what his interaction with his intellectual and affective environment make him.

The child's first dependence is on its mother, and with that idea I began this book. As the child develops its capacity to think, to speak, to act, it identifies with its family and quickly learns from it the ways of looking at things, of liking and disliking people and ideas, of accepting some attitudes and rejecting others. This is done here, and that is not done. This is the way we do it at home and this is the way it should be done everywhere. The child acquires its first coordinates. It knows what is good and what is bad in necessary landmarks for its incipient career.

While visiting in a friend's house I noticed that the TV was on in a corner and the small boy of the family was watching intently a program on election propaganda by rival political parties. When a speaker and his followers appeared on the screen, the boy asked his father, "Are these the good ones?" His father answered, "No, these are bad, but they are going to win." Brief lesson in political science. No argument and no discussion. The boy knows the name of the political party and knows that these are the bad guys. He also knows that the wrong party is going to win the elections. Political pessimism in early life. He will not argue with his father, will not ask for any reason or in any way question the verdict. These are the bad people and they are going to win. He knows. Daddy is always right. That is the view officially held in his family, and therefore also his own view. The family views become automatically his own because he belongs to the family, and acceptance of the family code is the unspoken but binding condition for the shelter and care he receives at home.

Dissent comes later. The boy grows up and finds that he is no longer in agreement with his parents. He wants freedom which is not granted, uses language which is not accepted, invites friends who are not welcome. He even disagrees now with his father, who, according to him, is an old-fashioned capitalist and does not understand the new needs of social justice and universal equality. Tension increases at home; the boy grows gradually silent, communication is almost nonexistent. That situation brings about an important change. The growing boy no longer finds his security at home; he does not trust his parents, feels they do not understand him, fears about his future at home. Yet he desperately needs security, and so he seeks it now in another group: his peer group. Surrounded by his friends, dressing as they dress and talking as they talk, he finds a new security and sticks to it with unflinching devotion. The parents are distressed and do not understand the sudden alienation of their fond child. They point out to him and to anyone who wants to listen to their plight that such a security among his peers is artificial, flimsy, ephemeral, treacherous; that the boy is much safer with his parents, who love him and have done so much for him and are ready to do much more, than with that assorted crowd of itinerant acquaintances, who will abandon him at the first trouble; that the boy is foolish and sees nothing now but will soon open his eyes and repent of what he is doing and will come back to trust his parents, who are the ones who love him best and want only what is best for him; and that the only thing they are afraid of is that by the time the boy comes back to his senses and again seeks his parents, it may be too late and irreparable harm may have been done.

It is hard for the parents to realize that their son feels safer with his companions than with them. It may even be absurd in itself, but it is a fact, and it is basic to understanding the workings of the young man's mind. He yearns for security and he finds it in being one in a crowd, in identifying with a group, in following fashion, in conforming to usage, in shouting common slogans and talking common slang. The crowd around him gives him a sense of security, false to be sure, but physical, tangible, experiential. He is never alone. He always moves around with others. In the street, on the campus, at games and parties, or just in idling and drinking, he is always surrounded by others like him who also seek support in the rest of them in a mutual pact that transforms several obvious weaknesses into an apparent strength. They all seek one another because they all are weak, and only together can they forget their weakness. Even at home he always has a phone close by for instant contact with others, who need it as much as he does. And then come the great "happenings" where thousands worship together at the altar of youth, and jump together and shout together and clap their hands together and screw their necks together at the same rhythm with the same music. Whatever else the young worshipers get out of those Bacchic liturgies, they do get a sense of belonging, of strength, of security, inspired by the sheer force of numbers in the surging crowd. We are in good company. In company, at any rate.

Sooner or later the young man realizes that the group does not give him the full safety he needs. He cannot go on forever moving around in a group and tousling his hair and fraying his pants. He has to settle somehow. He does so and thereby seeks safety in the institution. Financial security in a job, and affective security in marriage. Here it is not the visible crowd that surrounds him, but the secure bond of millions of people on earth who, like him, marry and hold a stable job. He fits the pattern and therefore feels at ease. He is part of the institution and heir to a tradition of centuries. History protects him, and the human race watches over him.

A secure job is both symbol and reality of the stability we all prize in life. It gives social standing, respectability, a designation on the visiting card, and an account in the bank. All these are constants in the life of modern man that outline his social profile and guarantee his welfare. In India people love to work in a bank, or rather, they do not like working in a bank (I cannot conceive of anybody liking to work in a bank), but they love to be able to say that they work in a bank. A bank is the ultimate symbol of safety and permanence in a society in which everything else seems to fail. The imposing building of the bank headquarters, the safe-deposit vault, the endless offices, the bundles of bank notes. To work in a bank is to live close to real money, to know the mysteries of human economic behavior, to finance and to insure and to lend and to advise. Business may collapse and industries may close down, but the bank remains. The safest job in the most permanent of institutions. Pride and satisfaction. Security for life. There is a good pension for all employees after a lifelong service. And the same is proportionally true of any job. Get a firm appointment and relax. You have something to do, somewhere to go, money to earn, and a position to boast of. No wonder even the most rebellious young men end up by filling in an application and signing up for a job. One has to be practical, after all.

One has to be practical and one marries also. For love, for children, for a family—and for a secure home, company, and care for life. Or, as in my case, one joins the religious life, and together with the divine call and the genuine desire to serve others and to belong fully to God, is there not also an unspoken need for quiet security to live free from worldly worries and material concerns? After all, life in a convent or a religious house is one of the most secure in this world and has a promise of eternal life in the next. The institution once again protects the individual and offers him proven ways and tried practices to live in peace with God and with men. I know well that religious life is a challenge and a risk, but I do not forget that it also is shelter and support.

Religion itself, in its beliefs and its practices, is not entirely lacking in an element of security that appeals to man in the uncertainties of his earthly existence. Together with pure love and selfless commitment, there is also the legitimate but inferior desire to make sure of God's approval in this life and in the next, and it is good to be aware of it. The religious institution confers security, and this is part of its contribution to human welfare. There is, however, a double danger in it: on the part of the subjects, to seek above all reassurance in their shakiness; and on the part of the authorities, to play on the need for security in order to ensure allegiance. I know gurus who promise salvation on conditions that vary from financial contributions to wearing and exhibiting their own image; and I know serious and intelligent and cultured people who give the money and worship the image to ensure salvation. Two needs have met here, with unhappy consequences: the need of the guru to have disciples, and the need of the disciples to have a guru. The guru is safe in his throne so long as the number of disciples increases, and the disciple is safe in his religious quest once he obtains the guru's blessing. Ultimately a matter of safety for both—and of credit to neither. True religion does not overemphasize safety as motivation.

I have mentioned that the search for safety becomes most acute at the two ends of human life, birth and old age. This is so because it is then that a person feels most his own helplessness. With old age come physical weakness, dependence on others, doubts about the past existence, and fear of what is to come. That is why old age witnesses again a return to the institution, to tradition, to conservative ideas and safe practices. It is no time for risks. As I was told by an old man who, after posing for many years as a practical atheist, had returned in his last years to belief and prayer, "You cannot afford to quarrel with the teacher when the exam approaches."

In a garden close to my residence, a group of very old men from our neighborhood meet every morning, and I often pass by their side in my walks and greet them. More than once I have also sat with them and exchanged thoughts. Once they read out to me some poems one of them had composed and all recited with gusto. This was the gist of one of them:

> When I was small, I held my mother's hand
> When I married, I leaned on my wife
> Now, when I am old, I lean on my walking stick
> I have never walked alone

Such is the human condition. Security is a walking stick. Welcome when needed, and dispensable when we feel strong. A walking stick helps us to walk—but not to run.

SMALL FEARS

I had forgotten to lock my bicycle. I had left it down in the street, leaning against the wall of the house where I was to spend the night. It was close to the door, but plainly unlocked for anyone to see. I remembered how it had happened. When I got down from the bike I saw the small girl of the family playing in the street, or rather, she saw me first, left her game at once, and came running to me with open arms. I had just time to steady the bicycle against the wall, turn to the girl, receive in my arms the sweet impact of her running body, lift her high to embracing height, and enter the house with her hands hugging my neck. Such a loving welcome had taken absolute preference over everything else, even over the elementary safety measure of locking the bicycle for the night. Thefts of bikes are unfortunately common, as everybody needs one, and it even provides a means of swift escape for the smart thief while the rightful owner is left on foot to curse his carelessness.

My bicycle was in good condition. It even had a light for night use, and so it was likely to attract the attention of any watchful collector of bikes. Those considerations made me uneasy as I turned in bed at night, unsuccessfully trying to sleep. My hosts had arranged for me to sleep on a balcony, as it was summer and the interior of the house was uncomfortably hot. I appreciated the gesture, though

I now realized the trouble it had posed for me. If I wanted to go down and lock my bicycle, I would have to pass through my hosts' bedroom, wake them up, and ask them to open the door for me. I swore to myself I would not do that. My hosts were most gracious, and since privacy in India is minimal, they certainly would not mind being disturbed and would go back to their sleep without a second thought. But I could not bring myself to shake them awake and plead for my bicycle in the dead of night. Better to lose the bike if it came to that. But still the problem remained: I could not sleep. My body was tossing fitfully on the rather thin mat on the floor of the balcony, but my mind was down in the street hanging on to my bicycle. Was it still there?

In my misery I turned to prayer. God was certainly aware of my plight; he knew I needed my sleep to rest for the night, and my bike to make my way to college next day in time for my classes. He was provident and powerful, and could surely watch over my bicycle, distract the attention of prowlers, and keep it safe for just one night. That is all I asked for. God certainly appreciated my trust in him and my delicacy toward my hosts. He would be true to his word, and the next morning I would rejoice at seeing his providence at work and my bicycle intact, and, of course, I would never again forget to lock it for the night. Now I could go safely to sleep. My fear of losing the bike had disappeared.

Yet sleep did not come. I thought now that I was using prayer as an escape. I could not sleep, and there was no sleeping pill available on the lonely balcony, so I had turned to prayer instead. I had brought in God to allay my fears. And now I felt that was an unworthy escape. If I had been foolish enough to leave my bicycle unlocked in the middle of the street during the night, I could not now bring God into that with a show of piety when all that was involved here was my insecurity and my forgetfulness. Let me suffer and learn from my mistakes. I searched my heart and found that I did not actually believe God could send his angels to watch over my bicycle and turn prospective thieves away. I was not sure what I would find next morning on the street; but now, at the edge of my sleep, prayer had provided for an instant cover and a much-needed psychological reassurance to pacify my mind and invite sleep. This thought disturbed me even more than the forlorn bicycle. I was using prayer to forget my anxiety instead of tackling my problem directly. Again, I lack the courage to wake up my hosts, and in a tour de force I appeal to God to set matters right with his omnipotent power. Not fair. God certainly helps me, but he expects me to do all that is in my hands. Let me think again and appraise the situation as it is.

There are two clear options before me: I do not disturb my hosts, I forfeit my sleep, and risk losing my bicycle; or I wake up my hosts, lock the bike, and finally get to sleep. When I set them out so clearly in my mind, the right choice becomes evident. After all, what keeps me from getting up and doing what's necessary is my own shyness and silly pride, making it almost impossible for me to admit that I can give trouble to others, when in fact I know that for them, this is no trouble at all. In fact, they will be much more distressed if tomorrow they find that my bicycle has been stolen while I was lodging with them. I feel ashamed to tell them now that I forgot to lock the bike, but I shall feel much worse if I have to confess to them tomorrow that it was stolen because I felt shy about telling them tonight. Crystal clear. Up with me, straight into their room, down to the street, and on to the bicycle. Fortunately it was still there. The whole impossible feat took a couple of minutes. We all went back to bed instantly, forgot about it, and slept soundly. The bicycle also slept soundly now. The lock was a strong one.

I learned some things that night. I could not sleep because I was afraid. When a tingle of fear enters the mind, it disturbs balances and shadows lights. Fear defeats peace. The frail harmony of the mind had been perturbed, and sleep would not come. Fear breaks the rhythm of nature and attacks the tissues of the body. Fear is born in the mind, but its influence is felt in nerves and muscles and pulse and breath. It makes a hungry man lose his appetite, and a sleepy man his sleep. No reasoning, no exercise, no soothing thoughts, and no lulling music will bring sleep to a fearful mind. The baleful effects of fear on the mind are signified and expressed by its effects on the body. Fear disturbs, cripples, unnerves. For physical and mental health, fear has to be banished from our minds. I also learned that often we tend to cover up our fear and attack only its symptoms, with the result that the roots remain and their harm continues and increases all the more behind the deceitful screen. We seek company, we distract the mind, we rationalize, we pray. All that is very good, but never as a substitute for facing the fear and working it out. Pushing down the fear without solving it is like sweeping under the carpet. The dirt remains, and if the practice continues, it will come out someday and cause more trouble when the heap of rubble is discovered and the carpet bursts with it. I felt glad, on reflection, that I could not sleep for a start that night. If I had succeeded, through willpower or a tranquilizer, in sleeping while the problem was still unsolved, I would have unconsciously stored a fear in my memory, and there is no more deadly stockpile of potential explosives than the stores of fear in the dark depths of our mind.

Small fears are not to be underestimated. They add up and create a psychosis of diffidence and instability. Big fears do not come up daily; it is the small ones that crop up in daily encounters with reality and undermine our power of resistance and growth. Fear of missing a train, of having parked badly, of not having written a check properly, of not having made sure all the faucets were closed. Fears with or without reason, with or without consequences, but always with one sinister consequence in the eroding of psychological defenses and mental health. We brush them aside when they come, we do not give them importance, we ignore them, but they sap our strength with the cancer of their secret anguish. Every unsolved fear is a burden on life. We have to uncover them, identify them, name them, and see them for what they are till we escape their grip and dissolve them in awareness and courage. Self-analysis will reveal that there are more fears in our cellar than we can number. They crowd together and reinforce each other, and when a bigger fear appears, they prepare the ground, accompany its tremors, and multiply its effect.

On the other hand, if we learn to unmask and tackle the small fears in daily skirmishes, we shall diminish their impact, and grow wiser and stronger to handle the more important fears that come along. To lose a bicycle is not a matter of life and death, but to realize that the fear exists, to let it surface, to watch it, to act in its face, and to clear the mind of all the dark residues it has left can be an exercise in sincerity and courage that builds up strength and readies the soul for fiercer battles in the cause of permanent peace. A lonely balcony under the friendly stars can become for a memorable night a school of wise living. Small apprehensions can be stepping-stones to understand and conquer the final enemy that is fear.

GETTING LOST

I looked carefully to check whether it was an illusion of mine or an actual fact. It was no illusion. His pants were shaking. All around his ankles, where the edge of his pants hung loose in well-ironed creases, the vertical wall of clothing was undulating like a flag in the wind. Only there was no wind. I wondered. He was an experienced speaker. He was standing in front of the microphone, his legs mercifully hidden by the upright lectern, and his speech was proceeding with his usual command of language, with flowing paragraphs and witty remarks, with apparent ease and instant communication. No one in the audience could guess the nervousness he was prey to while he spoke, but I was sitting behind him on the dais and could watch the comic ballet of his shaking legs. He finished his speech to a warm ovation. He stepped back and sat by my side. I turned to him and said, "Your legs were shaking." He replied, "They always do. That is why I never speak without a lectern. I cannot help it. I've learned to put up with the shaking, but I wish it were not there. I would speak with greater ease if I did not shake."

Stage fright. The best of speakers may feel a quiver of anxiety as he climbs onto the platform, receives the heat of the spotlight on his face and the glare in his eyes, and contemplates a multitude of people who look at him and are waiting for him to speak. There is the fear of forgetting an important point, of missing the link, of getting stuck, of not knowing how to end, and then the more chilling fear of not getting attention, of losing contact, of distractions and murmurs in the audience, of people getting up and leaving the hall. All this can happen, and the fear of it can freeze thought and paralyze speech. There are speakers who need to have before them the written speech or at least a detailed summary of it, even if they do not look at it during the performance. They need the physical presence, the reassuring paper, the written guarantee that the whole speech is there and they can always have recourse to it even if in fact they never do. Almost a superstitious ritual of private magic. The fetish must be at hand for ready worship. Only then can the ceremony succeed.

I find that the less tense I am, the better I function in public. If I am very keen on not forgetting a particular point, I am sure to forget it and to torture myself all the time while I keep on talking and keep on worrying desperately about which was the point I was so interested in bringing out and is now so hopelessly gone from my memory. It is miserable trying to be saying something to keep the speech going anyhow, and to be at the same time trying to rescue a forgotten thought from the unyielding darkness of a blank mind. There is a forced smile outside to emphasize a purported humorous point while free cursing is going on inside at the treacherous memory. The perfect way to ruin a speech. The listeners sense there is something wrong, though they cannot tell exactly what, as the speech proceeds uninterrupted, and their attention begins to stray. What is wrong is that the speaker is divided, his mind is not in his words, and so the words lack conviction and the spell is broken. Soon the audience will be distracted, chairs will move, eyes will wander, and that impossible situation will be created where the contact ceases and the speech becomes an empty sound over an alienated crowd. Anxiety to do well is the sure way to do badly.

The speech has to be prepared, to be sure, and that important point and the telling anecdote have to be carefully memorized and rehearsed to ensure as far as possible proper delivery at the proper moment. But after all this effort has taken place, one is to relax and even quietly accept the possibility that the speech may go flat and the cherished anecdotes may be lost on the audience. This is a difficult but delightful balance; to make on the one hand a full effort, to prepare each point and memorize each link, and then, on the other hand, to visualize a failure of communication and not be upset by it. To look at the audience with genuine desire of communication and intimacy, and to realize that this may not happen and then there is nothing to do about it. Full effort and full detachment. Full interest and full neutrality. And then a remarkable thing happens. When the fear of failure disappears by its very possibility being accepted, the mind becomes free, the ideas flow, the anecdotes are remembered at the proper time, and what is more, new anecdotes that had not been thought of come up now before the mind on their own and confer a new freshness and vitality to the speech. Thus paradoxically a scheme for the speech has to be carefully prepared . . . so that it can be abandoned when better ideas occur on the spot. Improvisation can take place only when there has been a careful preparation. The preparation gives confidence, the confidence frees the mind, and the free mind finds the right thing to say at the right moment in the actual delivery. Fearlessness is the basis of eloquence.

When Cicero defended Milo before Roman judges, he was afraid, as military allegiances were involved and he

felt unsure. The result was that his customary eloquence
left him, and though he was the best orator in the Roman
Empire, he spoke poorly, lost the case, and Milo was
exiled to Marseilles in Gaul. Mortified at his failure, Cicero
set about writing a new speech as he would have liked to
have it, a speech that was never delivered but has been
preserved and is considered an immortal classic in its
style. He sent a copy of the speech to Milo in Marseilles to
justify himself in a way and let his client know how he
would have liked to defend him, had he been himself at
the moment. Milo had a sense of humor, and after reading
the perfect oration, he wrote back to Cicero in Rome:
"Thank God you did not give this speech on that day,
otherwise I would be missing the excellent fish I am eating
here." The bouillabaisse of Marseilles seems to have had a
long tradition. Cicero had actually done a clever thing in
that second speech. He had listed at the beginning of it the
reasons that made him afraid, and had refuted them one
by one as though to convince himself and strengthen
himself. That was a trick. He knew those same reasons
were making the judges afraid, as they were chiefly fear of
government and of the military, who wanted Milo condemned, and so in refuting them for himself, he was
refuting them for the judges, and in telling himself to have
courage, he was, indirectly and tactfully, telling the judges
to be fearless. That sounds beautiful and convincing, but it
is only in the speech that was never delivered.

It is easier to show courage on paper than before a high
court bench. A person can easily tell others why they
should not be afraid, while all the time being afraid for the
same reasons. So afraid was Cicero that he could not even
bring himself to expose those reasons on that day, and his
speech was so poor that he destroyed all records of it while
he made sure that copies of the second speech would be

filed for posterity. We now possess a model speech, and a signal testimony of what fear can do to a great man.

Writers are also prey to a special kind of fear, not so well known but familiar to me in my spells of writing. I was consoled when I read the declarations of a great writer, Salman Rushdie, to an Indian paper. In them he described the crisis he lived through when planning and tackling a new book, and I could smile to myself, recognizing kin fears. He said that when he chose the theme for a new book, he felt sure and confident he had more than enough matter to fill a long volume, and the only problem would be to choose ideas and organize the plot. When he started writing, however, he was suddenly paralyzed by a chilling fear. He was afraid he did not have enough to write about, he would get stuck in the middle, and would never be able to finish the book for lack of material. He panicked and froze, and was unable to write for a time. Then he finally got around to writing again, the work proceeded smoothly, and in the end he found indeed that he had enough matter and some to spare. I know the trial. The initial enthusiasm, the sudden panic, the slow relief. It was an irrational fear, the initial plans were clearly sufficient, the file with notes for the future book was filled to capacity, the mind was eager to get into its creative mood, which is the last and only guarantee of the flow of writing. But the thought was blocked by an insane fear, and the work was stayed. The hand would not move and the mind would not work. It takes all the desperate courage of the act of literary creation to break the barrier and start the flow again. Labor pains at the birth of originality in a world of repetition. Another great Indian writer, V. S. Naipaul, tells how he wrote his first book: "I never numbered my pages, for fear of not getting to the end" (*Finding the Center*).

Lope de Vega wrote the best-known sonnet in Spanish literature by toying with each verse in the fear that he would not reach the next. It is a filigree of delicate feeling, affected fear, subtle humor, nursed cadences, and perfect rhyme. He begins under orders, despairs of ever completing the errand, makes real the apprehension that the work may stop at any moment and remain unfinished, conquers one by one the repeated summit of the looming verse, lets the suspense pile up, embarks with graceful ease on the venture of the next line, conquers one more rhyme, varies each approach with the renewed challenge, squares his achievement, and presents with a flourish the fourteen-verse wonder to the teasing beauty who had asked for it. A poet can also know fear, and experience the rewards of overcoming it.

Orchestra conductors have also confessed to stage fright. For all their glamour, their art, their identification with pure sound, and their power to turn to thrill and beauty the coded cipher of captive notes, they feel the presence of the audience, the challenge of the orchestra, the weight of history, the risk of a fiasco, the loneliness of the podium, and they suffer in their souls while they make real, in the midst of silence, the most sublime masterpieces humans have ever created. It all looks safe and secure in the most elegant of settings, but it is not. There is fear and diffidence and nervousness. Bernstein revealed that before each piece, he had to bodily touch the score, glance through it even if seeing nothing, hold it and press it in his hands, and only then could he walk on the stage and wield the baton.

Conducting without a score is no mean feat. Mahler's Third Symphony takes a full orchestra, a children's choir, and a soprano the best of two hours to perform. And each note of the unconventional score, each entry, each modulation, has to be infallibly remembered and promptly acted upon for a flawless performance. The conductor cannot afford a hesitation, a delay, a false cue. That would ruin the show. Yet the burden on his memory must not tell on the freedom of his art, and the worry of the mind must not hinder the sweep of the baton. I know some music by heart and can still play Mozart's Sonata in C Major (KV 545) without too many mishaps, but then its charmingly simple Alberti accompaniment of unfolded chords on the left hand almost plays itself out and the fingers do the job without bidding. Quite another matter is the complex score of a modern composition with its heavy demands on ear, eye, and memory.

André Previn, no mean conductor himself, discloses the secret that all conductors, even the best ones, get lost at times while conducting their orchestras. A false step, a distraction, a blacking out, and the conductor wonders where he stands while the orchestra goes on playing unconcernedly as though a conductor was not needed after all. André Previn's advice to his fellow conductors, drawn from his own experience, is not to try desperately to catch up with the orchestra or in any way force the players to come to where the conductor thinks they should be, but to relax, to let them play, to make general movements with his arms which could fit any rhythm, and to wait for the rendezvous that will take place sooner or later without the audience having realized at all that anything went wrong. The fear of getting lost and the anxiety to get back into beat as soon as possible are only a hindrance to regaining control. Relax and take it easy. Have a sense of humor and enjoy getting lost. It is also an enlightening experience worth going through. At the end, the concert is always a success and people clap for an encore.

Life is also a symphony, and we all get lost in it at times. The score is complicated; there are difficult passages, daring solos, and imposing tuttis. We lose the rhythm at times and do not seem to know when and how all this will end. Never mind. Do not panic. Let the music go on. We are sure to get into it again and the show will be great. Music never fails.

STANDING ERECT

Anthropologists say that humans began to walk erect because they were afraid. Most large animals on land walk on four legs. Even apes that favor their hind legs for prompt displacement lean also on their forelegs in a jump-and-run trot when they are not hanging from the branch of a tree or swinging happily with flying grace from treetop to treetop. Humans alone walk erect. We have even come to see in our exclusive deportment a sign of our superiority, dignity, and nobility. We alone look up to heaven, we alone can turn our heads to all sides, we alone keep our hands free from the dust of the ground on which we walk. People who walk erect proclaim their confidence and their strength, and to walk with a stoop is a sign of weakness even among people. We are proud of our stand, and consider it our privilege and our glory. To the first ape that stood up on its way to human evolution we even gave the name of *Pithecanthropus erectus,* making its erect stand *(erectus)* the dividing line between ape *(pithecos)* and human *(anthropos).*

In reality, things are not so glorious. The honest fact is that we stood up because we were afraid. We did not have much in the way of defenses in the middle of the jungle. We could not boast of the strength of the lion or the speed of the deer, we did not have the wings of the eagle or the poison of the snake. We had only the first spark of human intelligence, which enabled us to foresee, to plan, and to protect ourselves. The first thing our intelligence did for us was to warn us of dangers and prompt us to ward them off. The attack in the jungle may come from any quarter, and so it was essential for the Hairless One (in Rudyard Kipling's description) to be able to look around swiftly, to turn his head to the four quarters, and focus instantly with two-eyed vision on any shadow or any movement, far or near. An animal on all fours has a limited field of vision and cannot look back without turning its whole body. Man on his feet has only to turn his head slightly to watch any corner, and that was the primal motivation to get on his feet and walk erect. Man needed protection from the dangers his intelligence had told him existed all around, and began to walk straight to be able to look over his shoulder. Intelligence that makes him a man, fear that comes from the dangers his intelligence points out to him, and the erect stand to ward off those dangers, those are the stages of our evolution.

The bullocks, in Rudyard Kipling's dialogue, can draw guns into battle without feeling fear because "they only see in front of them" and "they cannot see inside their heads." Their human captain, on the contrary, "can see things inside his head before the fire begins, he can see inside his head what will happen when a shell bursts, and he shakes all over." This ability to "see things inside our heads" is what gets us into trouble in the battlefield. Fear is born of our capacity to imagine the future. Our intelligence made us cautious and put us on our guard against the dangers that threatened our existence. And so man became a watchtower in his own body, tall and straight, to scour the horizon for any sign of danger in the treacherous jungle. Thus man, the Hairless One, could survive and establish his supremacy over all other animals. This "seeing inside our heads" has its advantages also, and though it brought fear, it also brought us our privileged position on earth. To that exclusive faculty we owe, for better or for worse, our species habit of standing erect.

Our orthopedic surgeons know well how much that habit has cost us. Our spine, which in animal bodies was never meant to stand upright, has to take a lifelong punishment that wears out vertebrae, squeezes out cartilages, stiffens necks, and cripples nerves. It is not conducive to health for an earthly body to walk on two legs, to stand upright for hours on end, to let the weight of the whole body hang on the spine, to defy daily and throughout a lifetime the one cosmic universal law that ultimately conquers us and literally weighs us down, the law of gravity. We would be so much more comfortable and healthy romping about on all fours, close to the earth that bore us and with the horizontal bearing nature recommends to all its children on land and sea. When we were small we moved that way and enjoyed ourselves immensely till well-meaning adults coaxed us and forced us with enticements and encouragement to learn how to walk as they did, and with that, to fall, to be hurt, to stand unnaturally, and to feel uncomfortable for the rest of our lives. Wise animals learn by themselves how to walk, and do so almost immediately after birth; we, wisest of them all, wait for years, learn slowly, and need the help of others. They follow nature's way, while we choose to stand erect in a flat world, and we pay heavily for our originality. Any X-ray photograph of the back of an adult will show to the trained eye the telltale signs of the passage of time. "Spondylitis," the doctor will say, and will add with a reassuring tone, "normal at your age." Yes, normal for men and women of my age, but I am sure that if an X ray is taken of a healthy horse or a philosoph-

ical cow of comparable age, it will show no spondylitis of
any kind. At least I do not know of cows and horses
wearing orthopedic belts or neck supports, as men and
women do in increasing numbers. Nor of their being
operated upon for slipped disks. Penalty for our pride.

Living in India, my body experiences the consolation of
being able to sit on the floor, cross-legged on soft matting,
leaning back on the wall in the wise comfort of Oriental
etiquette. Chairs are spurned, sitting upright is martyr-
dom, tables are instruments of torture. The body loves the
mattress on the floor, the large round pillow behind,
the spread-out legs, the bare feet, the resting elbow, the
relaxed back. The lower the body, the happier the mind.
The West wants people to think of heaven, and draws out
the head high into the air to make them look up and see
the clouds; the East knows that the best way to get to
heaven later is to be solidly on earth now, and so it invites
people to sit low and lie down. The leisurely, literally
down-to-earth posture practiced in the East is part and
instrument of the internal peace that is the core of spiritual
tradition and endeavor in this part of the world. People
are restored to their earthly sources.

The upright position of humans, then, with their inferiority and their dominance, comes originally from the fear
their intelligence uncovered for them. This means that fear
is inscribed in our bones and quavers in our marrow every
time we stand up and turn our heads. We carry with us the
imprint of our ancestry. Our body forms part of our fears.
The machinery that sets us trembling is not only our imagination gone wild but also our organism remembering its
history. The chemistry of our bodies reinforces the
thoughts of our mind. We know that well in our own
experience. A sudden fear triggers a hormonal reaction that
quickens the pulse and alerts the senses. Our fears are felt

in our whole organism. This realization can help us to understand them better and control them in part. We know that we have to think of our body if we want to keep our fears in check.

Recently I was in a huge supermarket when suddenly all the lights went off. There was total darkness except for a few fluorescent arrows to indicate the emergency exits. The large crowd was stunned for an instant, and panic could be sensed in the dark. I visualized for a fleeting moment how a catastrophe could happen. A scream, a stampede, a dash for safety, ignoring the similar claim of all around, and the crowded store could have become a death trap for many. There was terror in the air. The lights came back as suddenly as they had gone, and revealed frightened faces and strained postures. And then a universal sigh of relief emerged at the same time from a hundred throats, and smiles came back to paralyzed bodies. The whole dark space had for a moment been the abode of fear. The body in its tenseness, its taut nerves, its held breath, its palpitations, its adrenaline, had suddenly created a space of fear in the close boundary. The reaction had been quick, and the panic instant. And so was the release from the tension. Breathing became normal, muscles relaxed, voice returned to the somber room. The specter of fear had touched the unsteady crowd. Business continued as usual.

Fear causes us to "hold our breath," and repeated fears, big and small, day and night, through conscious and subconscious channels, with their lingering, their forebodings, their imprint, and their shadow, engender in us the permanent disability of shallow breathing, which is one of the most damaging habits for our mental and bodily health. Shallow breathing, Thérèse Bertherat says, is like living in a six-room house and occupying only one room. A waste of space and of energy.

The breath we take in is called in Sanskrit *prana* (life), and so the less air we breathe, the less life we live. Oxygen is given to us freely, and we, with a show of altruistic politeness, take only a small portion of it and leave the rest literally hanging in the air, frustrated in its original purpose of giving life. A deep breath fills the lungs, steadies the body, clears the mind, gives peace. Short breaths keep us panting in the physical anxiety of a body gasping for life and in the mental anguish of a frightened mind begging for support. And then the vicious circle sets in. Fear had made us hold our breath, and now this impoverished breath in turn keeps us in suspense and increases our fears. Our defective breathing is responsible not only for our decreased vitality, but also for our increased fearfulness. This realistic warning can become a help in reducing our fears once we understand how the body, which had been adversely affected by a tense mind, can now, by itself initiating the healing process with its self-possession and its regularity, bring back to the mind the serenity that is meant to reside in the whole organism for its integrated development.

If fear tenses my muscles and shortens my breath, I can, by calming my breath and loosening my muscles, invite peace again into my threatened system. Fear cannot coexist with relaxed muscles and quieted breathing. The mind cannot be troubled while the body is at peace. If I have no direct access to my mind to free it from the apprehensions, terrors, and worries that grip it, I can always work through the body, calm my breath, relax my posture, unwind my muscles, smile, and present to the world again a friendly face instead of the contorted mask that panic had clamped on me. It's a simple exercise, with quick and noticeable results. The calm of the body works itself into the calm of the mind. Slow your pace, control your movements, modulate your voice, steady your eyes, walk and speak and act as a calm, serene, self-possessed person would speak and act. Little by little the calm will permeate the body and the brain with friendly, intimate steps toward the heart and the mind, and fear will ease its grip on your conscience. Body and mind will demonstrate their partnership in the willingness of their mutual influence and their reciprocal training.

This training may look a little artificial, and may even take a bit of acting at the beginning. Our spontaneous reaction, even a misguided sincerity to appear as we are, may urge us to appear outside as we are inside. Let my body register the state of my mind without any veil or censorship. If I am nervous, let me appear nervous and let all see that I am nervous and know me as I am. This may be fine as a public confession, but need not be the best way to heal my excessive nervousness. I can proceed in another quite legitimate and more efficient way. If I am nervous, I can, with a little practice, begin to act as though I were not; I can speak with a steady voice, fix my eyes, and direct my hands with grace and poise so that in a very short while I myself will sense calm inside me and will see it reflected in those in front of me, and their witness will reassure me in my peace. A body without tensions houses a soul without fears.

Let us not allow our bodies to become prey to the symptoms of fear. If we are to walk erect, as we are not likely to give up now the doubtful privilege of our haughty stance, we can do so in the awareness of our body and the suppleness of our muscles, in the gracefulness of our movements and the alertness of our senses, in the firmness of our step and the friendliness of our gaze, and never in the hurry, the suspicion, the flight, the hunched back, the wary look, the whispered threat, the shaking gait, of bodily fear. Let us drop once and for all the ancestral fear that still runs in our blood since the far-off days when our ancestors lived in the savage jungle. We have enough fears to worry us in our own jungle without being burdened with those of other landscapes and other days. Sufficient unto the age is the evil thereof.

THE GOOD LUCK NECKLACE

Financial insecurity. For many of us only words. At most a concept. We know, of course, that there are people who do not know how the sum of money they receive at the beginning of the month is going to last until the end, who are not sure when the income will cease to come at all, and who have no resources to draw from in an emergency of bodily sickness or social need. But we have not experienced in our own flesh the shame of the unpaid bill, the anguish of the approaching date, the repeated misery of the counting of money to see how far it can reach, the ruthless budget, the impossible account, the stubborn gap. The silence of the wife in her heroic thrift, the unsatisfied children, the minimal expenses, the worn-out clothes, the insufficient meals. And the cruel uncertainty that even this may not last because circumstances are difficult, the job is uncertain, retrenchment is coming, and nobody knows on whom the axe will fall. How to live with this situation day by day in a poor house with old furniture, precious all the same for him who has nothing else to call his own, fearing an eviction, a sickness, the inability to pay the fees for his children to study, the prospect of things getting even worse as things are not easy and misery increases on all fronts. Such daily nightmare is the hardest trial that can be conceived for a person who otherwise has to put up a front, smile as though all were well, encourage his children, and show himself confident and cheerful in his work. God knows what his heart suffers while his face smiles.

Once I accidentally met on the street a man I had not seen for quite a few years. He recognized me first, came up to me, and renewed the acquaintance. Then I remembered. He was the owner of a small restaurant in a street where I had lived for some time, and the old warmth returned fast while we renewed all links talking in the middle of the crowded street, standing precariously and being pushed around by impatient passersby. I asked him about his business. His face fell visibly and he lowered his voice. He informed me that he had initially let the restaurant be registered under the name of his partner, whom he fully trusted but who had taken advantage of that trust and gone to court against him and expelled him from the partnership. My friend and his family were now suffering real want in abject poverty. I looked at him more carefully and I saw the marks of poverty. His coat was worn-out and showed several ill-disguised stains. His eyeglasses were glued. His teeth had not seen a dentist for years. He was the image of a man who tries hard to keep a decent front with utmost thrift.

He spoke briefly and without self-pity, keeping his nobility of character in the midst of the indigence in which he now lived. Then his face lit up slightly and he said, "Maybe our difficulties will come to an end now. There is the possibility of my getting a job in Bombay. Actually, you meet me here now because I am coming from the railway station, where I had gone to find out the price of the cheapest ticket to Bombay. The problem is"—and here his face grew somber again—"that all the money we have at home does not reach even to half that amount. I don't know what I shall do."

The words of that sincere man in his obvious sorrow brought a deep sadness to me as I watched him and sensed his pain. The price of a rail ticket to Bombay is not more than what a simple meal costs in a modest hotel. And when all the money in that house had been counted, when all the drawers had been searched and all the pockets had been emptied, when all the coins had been piled together and counted and recounted, the sum did not come even to half of the amount required. How can people live like that? Several mouths to feed and bodies to clothe, house rent to be paid and school fees to be met. And no money for it. Day after day and month after month. And now comes this golden opportunity of the beckoning job. Almost within reach. But no cash for the trip. And I think ahead. Even the job is not sure. The trip may be in vain, or another trip will be necessary, or initial expenses if he gets a new job. Where is all that to come from? And all along the specter of insecurity haunting each step. Will the job come? Will it last? Will luck hold? Shall we go back to a greater misery? I lived for a moment, in the presence of that unfortunate man, the agony of a person who is short of cash for urgent needs. What that state of insecurity can be like when it is prolonged for a lifetime is beyond our imagining.

The best story of the Gujarati writer Kisansingh Chavada, reprinted in all anthologies, included in all textbooks, and asked about in all examinations, is a true story of his own experience as a young man. He was young and jobless, and his mother was a widow. They had enough to live modestly, but as he grew up, the need increased to find a job and get a secure position for himself and his mother and his future family. He had to start somewhere. He inquired here and there and got a first offer as a newspaper vendor. A small job, but something to begin with.

The only snag was that a bicycle was essential for the job, and he did not have one. The boy mentioned the matter indifferently to his mother, and forgot about it. No bicycle, no job; that was the upshot of it, so he would keep on watching for other opportunities. But his mother knew what that first job would mean for her son, and her mind started working as only a mother's mind can work. Every Hindu wife owns a special wedding ornament called the *mangal sutra* (literally, the "good luck necklace"), which she receives on her wedding day and keeps jealously till the day of her death. It is her most priceless possession. It signifies her fidelity to her husband, the fertility of her marriage, and the well-being of her family under the protection of God, who blessed her marriage and protects her as woman and wife and mother. A visible sign of femininity at its best. A treasure exclusive to women, and which no man can own. It must of necessity have some gold in it, even just a little bit in the case of the woman who is not rich. But the touch of precious metal is there to signify the unique value of beauty and womanhood in the heart of the family. Only if she becomes a widow will the woman remove her necklace, and even then she will keep it in its case to guard her fidelity to her husband in his death as in life. The ornament is not for trade, its emotional value being much more than its market value, whatever this may be.

Yet it was to that unique and treasured possession that the boy's mother turned now as a last resource. She did not say anything, sure that she would be stopped in her plans, but she acted.

The next day the boy found at the door a brand-new bicycle, and to his joyful astonishment, his mother told him it was his for keeps. The boy did not know much then of the ways of life, but he thought and reached the

dreaded conclusion. Could she have. . . ? He knew the
meaning and the value of the "good luck necklace," knew
that it could never be alienated and that, whatever the
circumstances, that would be the last thing his mother
would do. Yet he could not think of another way in which
that bicycle could have come home. Finally the innocent
boy asked the loving mother. Had she perhaps . . . ? The
mother, with serene self-control born of her very love for
her only child, let her head speak while she silenced her
feelings. What was the use of a piece of jewelry in a box,
when it could become a useful bicycle for both of them to
live? Was that not what the boy's father would have
wanted? What better use of the idle gold than to make it a
means of livelihood, of work, the beginning of a life of
honest toil? Actually, as the widowed mother went on to
explain, she was now relieved not to have to keep gold in
the house, with the nuisance it was and the danger it
entailed. Was not the necklace meant to bring safety and
happiness to the family, and was it not doing it now rather
belatedly but in a most concrete and perceptible manner?

The mother won. The boy took his bicycle with a
reverence as though the whole of it were made of gold,
and went on with it to work, to become a man, to treasure
in his heart the priceless heritage of a wise and selfless
mother. And when the boy became a man, and the
newspaper vendor a writer, he wrote his best story ever
on that living memory that had shaped his life. He called
it "Mangal Sutra," and with that sacred name it made its
way into the literary anthologies and the appreciative
hearts of all thoughtful readers in Gujarat.

We feel close to the brave mother in her sacrifice
because we imagine to some extent the courage needed to
live day to day in dire financial straits. To spend the last
money, to take a bold gamble, to be left in the nagging

uncertainty of tomorrow, not to mention the distant future. The fear of not being able to support oneself and one's family is, in all its materiality, a burden only too real to many people in many climates, and not only to the openly destitute, but to many others who behind apparent economic ease lead lives of thrift and penury which make for constant worries and tense relations at home. The insurance business plays an important part in the economy of any developed country, and its very basis is the need people have to feel secure. The really poor people, however, cannot afford insurance, and live their daily insecurity in faith or fatalism, in protest or resignation, in oblivion or despair. No insurance can cover the harm done to the mind by a continued condition of economic want with no solution at hand.

AFFECTIVE INSECURITY

A sensitive soul prayed: Lord, I do not pray for myself; I can say without boasting that I will put up with the crosses you may send me; I can bear that. What I find unbearable is to see people close to me and dear to me suffer; for them I pray to you; spare them, Lord, for their sake and for mine.

Such generous prayer opens up one more front of vulnerability for our minds. We are liable to feel insecure now, not only for ourselves, but also and very seriously for those we hold in love and esteem. Their danger is our danger, their hurt is our hurt. And often, as the person who uttered that prayer, we are more apprehensive about the sufferings that may come to others than to ourselves. We feel we can manage somehow, while the other person is so frail and delicate that we cannot bear the thought of seeing him or her suffer. The burden of love is that by taking others to our heart, we take also their trials and dangers, and so we increase the range of our insecurity. Blessed burden, of course, but not to be ignored or minimized in our search for the roots of our fear.

I was visited by a married couple whose only son had won a scholarship to a renowned university in a far-off place, and the anxious parents were of two minds about the desirability of their son accepting the offer or not. They wanted me to list the dangers, but I preferred to let their own fears surface. They had heard of loose morals on the campus, of sex, of drugs. Their son was an exemplary young man who knew only the innocent world of the peasant village. He was good at studies and regular at his work, and could be expected to do well in the line he had chosen. He was a young man of promise. But what would happen to him in the unfriendly town? The greatest fear was that he would never come back. He could meet with an accident. Or he could do very well in his studies, get enticing offers, and go abroad. Or he could marry a heady girl and never return home. It was deeply painful to hear his good mother, with her wrinkled face and her honest thinking, express one by one the concrete fears that burdened her heart. Her son was her greatest treasure, pride of her village, hope of her family, security in her old age. Now all that was at stake. How could she let him go? On the other hand, how could she hold him back, cut his progress, and ruin his future? That would be unforgivable selfishness. The son would go. And the mother would live in the long anxiety of her lost security. Whatever happens to the child is a threat to the mother. Every letter will be opened with trembling hands, and every long period without a letter will be a silent agony of dark presentiment. Distance increases the insecurity felt by those who love from afar.

A mother confides that her growing daughter does not now speak to her about herself. She has become silent, secretive, aloof. She avoids any inquiries and ignores questions about herself. She behaves well at home and is careful in her dealings with all, but she keeps to herself, and no one at home knows what is going on now in her mind and in her life. This was not so before, and the mother wonders what is happening. She is afraid. So far she could control her daughter because she knew all that she did and thought. Now the link has been broken, she has lost control, and she is afraid. What will happen to my daughter if I can no longer protect her? And how can I protect her if she is not open with me? And does not the very fact that she is not open with me prove clearly that something is wrong with her? If everything were right with her, she would talk as she did before, but now she has locked her lips because there is something she does not want to be revealed. The uneasiness grows and the fear increases. And the fear further entangles the twisted relationship. The daughter senses the mother's fear and closes up all the more. Maybe she was talking less of late simply because of adolescent confusion, of growing bewilderment, of the newly discovered value of personal privacy; but now she knows her mother's suspicion, and that makes her grow suspicious herself. Fear engenders fear, and communication stops. The process is clear, but is difficult for a loving mother to understand. The daughter's estrangement makes the mother feel insecure, and the whole family suffers for it.

Insecurity with respect to the welfare of a person we love makes us suffer, and when the insecurity extends itself to our very relationship with that person, it can cause much more intimate suffering. I love my friend, value his friendship, enjoy his company, and rejoice in the thought that our intimacy will last forever. But then one day suspicion creeps in. He does not come now so often. He sounds distant. He gets distracted. Is he growing cold? Have I done anything that has displeased him? Has he another friendship that he finds more satisfying? Am I losing him? I begin to feel insecure about him, and react by becoming possessive. I do not want to lose him, and so, in my fear of losing him, I grab him.

Now, this is the worst thing that can happen to our

friendship. Possessiveness grown out of insecurity. I want to make sure he is not going to go away, and I coax, I persuade, I bring pressure, I make demands. And he, obviously, resents it. Our friendship was based on mutual freedom, on confidence and trust, and now, all of a sudden, I become suspicious, irrational, exacting. He sees it at once, and precisely because our friendship was delicately shaped and finely tuned, it jars now all the more on him, and now he truly begins to feel estranged from me. Maybe my first suspicion was just imagination, maybe it was just a spell of affective fatigue as is felt in the best of relationships, maybe it was a passing cloud; but now my fear and insecurity have made it into a major conflict. My insecurity has been communicated to him and has triggered a similar reaction in him. Now he feels insecure about me and my friendship. Mutual mistrust develops while I think the first symptoms showed in him and he thinks they showed in me. The situation is all the more difficult to resolve as it does not have a concrete cause that could be pointed out, discussed, and cleared up. An insecure relationship will sooner or later run into trouble.

On the contrary, a basic security, within the vicissitudes of the unpredictable human heart, is the best foundation for a lasting friendship. I know my friend, I understand his moods, I respect his silences, I have learned that longer absences build up closer reunions provided I do not fret about them, question him, and doubt his sincerity. Temporary withdrawals are a normal part of the closest of relationships, and they should not become a ground for suspicion but a school of greater intimacy. I can wait, I am steady, I do not grow mistrustful, I do not retaliate with studied aloofness. I let him free, precisely because I know he loves me, and in being himself, he will find in himself his love for me. This is the opposite of possessiveness, of moral domination and affective tyranny. Freedom as the basis of love, and lack of fear as the basis of freedom.

The following example may sound comic now, but not so when it happened quite some time ago. A married woman came to tell me she wanted to divorce her husband, and after my usual patient questioning to find out the seriousness of the situation and explore possible solutions, she very clearly expressed the final motive that had led her to her radical decision: "I want to divorce him now because I am afraid he may divorce me first." Preemptive tactics. I am afraid that he may strike first, so I steal a march on him and act first. She needed secrecy for the plan, of course, and I certainly was not going to say a word, but attitudes communicate, thoughts speak, and plans betray themselves, and in all probability the husband had sensed his wife's fears and might well be planning a similar move: let me file a divorce suit against her before she files it against me. Each acts out of the fear that the other is going to act, and in all probability if that fear were not there, neither of the two would get started at all.

Insecurity breeds insecurity, fear reinforces fear, and in the end two people who could well have sorted out their differences in reasonable dialogue find themselves confronting one another in a court of law. Many homes have been wrecked by an initial insecurity that was not uncovered and tackled in time. Trust is an essential part of love.

THE ART OF CONCENTRATION

This is to me one of the important lessons in life, and it can be easily stated. The secret of doing things well is concentration. Fear precludes concentration. Therefore fear is eminently responsible for our doing things poorly, unworthily, below our possibilities, and against our own legitimate expectations. Fear is the great spoiler.

Concentration is the soul of excellency in work. A person may have intelligence, imagination, power, and training, but if he does not concentrate himself at the moment of working, his intelligence will not show and his powers will not be used to the full. Concentration is the lens that focuses the dispersed faculties of the mind on the one dot that is the single point under consideration at the moment, and brings to act upon it all the thought, the experience, the creativity, that together make light and kindle the flame of understanding in the thrill of discovery. Geniuses are proverbially absentminded; that is, they are so much concentrated on their own thoughts that they disregard the practical conventionalities of common usage. Concentration on their speciality prevents them from paying attention to routine details of daily life, and their innocent gaffes provide laughing matter to their admirers, who rejoice to see that their heroes are, after all, human. On the contrary, a neurotic is simply defined as a self-interrupter, a walking distraction, a person who, for all his

brains and abilities, cannot concentrate on anything and
butterflies his way through life without any single achievement worth notice. Concentration is the condition of
efficiency in any activity and in any enterprise.

The story is told of Kant that one day he could not
conduct his class because one of the students was wearing
a red vest. The philosopher began this class like every
other, with the repeated rituals that facilitated concentration and led up to the rarified heights of the most abstract
thinking. He doffed his hat, rested his stick, adjusted his
chair, cleared his throat, began to speak short phrases
with long pauses, while his eyes surveyed the familiar
view of walls, benches, faces. There he stopped. Something was disturbing the routine, breaking the pace,
jarring the senses. There it was. The bright, glaring,
aggressive red color of a student's vest. The professor
tried again. He began a new sentence, a fresh look, a
leisurely scanning of the classroom landscape. All went
well until the red landmark. There it was again. How
could one proceed with subtle reasonings when that red
flag was blocking every attempt at organized thought? The
student, of course, was unaware of the intellectual havoc
his new vest was creating in the professor's mind, and the
whole class was wondering what was happening today
that things were not clicking and the lesson was not
getting started. The professor tried his best, until finally,
with the humility that accompanies all truly great men, he
pointed at the offending color that blocked his thought.
That was a good lesson by itself. Without concentration,
even the greatest philosopher of his time could not put
order in his thoughts to deliver the carefully prepared
lecture. And what a frail thing concentration is when a red
vest in a closed classroom is enough to break it!

In India there is a bird, whose name I have not learned,

that emits through its throat a low hissing sound as of a deflating balloon. That is its cry or song, and the fact that I did not know it got me into trouble at the beginning of my teaching career. I was addressing my mathematics class of one hundred boys and girls with the best brains in the country and a bursting eagerness to learn as much as possible in as short a time as possible. My enthusiasm matched theirs, and I enjoyed my classes because of the quickness of their understanding and the sharpness of their reactions. I was cautious, however, as one hundred students is a large number and mathematics is an abstract subject, and the slightest distraction can ruin the best theorem. I enforced pin-drop silence, rapt attention, no liberties, no interruptions. Only in that climate of total concentration could I do justice to myself, my subject, and my students.

One day, while I was working out a delicate demonstration on the blackboard with my back to the class, I heard in the midst of the total silence the incongruous noise of a deflating balloon. I froze. What mischief-maker dared to profane my class with that vile joke? I looked back in a flash. The whole student body was unmoved. Had it been a hallucination of mine? The whole class was unstirred. I continued with a self-willed effort. And then again the noise. Clear, slow, irritating. Who the hell could he be? I went on somehow, waiting to catch the culprit red-handed. The noise came a third time and I exploded. I told my class that if that was the way they chose to behave, they could just as well go and find another teacher for themselves, that mathematics was too serious and too sacred a subject to be treated with such levity, that they knew perfectly well who the miscreant was, and that unless he confessed and apologized, I would not continue my class or engage any other class.

It was a nice speech on the whole, with the proper intonation, indignation, and finality in my wounded dignity, and the students listened to it with awed reverence. But then, horror of horrors, while I was delivering my extempore speech, the bird spoke again. I bellowed, "Who is doing that to my own face?" Silence and downward looks. I was getting ready to call the Holy Inquisition when a girl in the front row, with a courage beyond her age, got up and said demurely, "Sir, it is a bird." Indeed. A bird. The girl pointed with her hand, through the door that had remained open because of the heat, to the ceiling of the open corridor that ran the length of the college wing. I followed her finger, got down from the platform, and walked into the corridor to face the evidence. There it was. The bird looked at me, opened its beak, and emitted its family call. So that was it. Perfect demonstration. I waved the bird away and it flew through the door of the next classroom, where I hoped the teacher knew more about Indian fauna than I knew. I went back to my class and I spent the rest of the time in a question-and-answer period. The link had been broken and I could not go back to my well-rehearsed program. And a lurking suspicion has remained in my mind to this day that some nonmathematically inclined boys planted the bird that day outside my classroom.

G. H. Hardy was, besides a great mathematician, a great lover of cricket. His friend C. P. Snow endeavored to prevail on him to write a book on his unusual knowledge and experience of the game. The title of the book was to be *One Day at the Oval*. They even discussed the chapters and points it would contain, but the book was never written. One of the ancedotes that would have gone into the book does remain, however, and reveals the playful character of the serious man who lived it. A test match Hardy was witnessing had to be interrupted because the batsman's eyes were dazzled by someone directing a sharp ray of light on them. On a sunny day anybody with a small mirror held in the proper position can focus the sun's reflection into the eyes of a distant person and dazzle him out of vision. Somebody was doing that to the batsman on the crease, and the game could not proceed so long as the disturbance remained. The umpire duly stopped the game and ordered a discreet inquiry into the incident so that its cause could be promptly removed. The trouble was that the likely area in the stands from where the obnoxious light could come coincided with the benches reserved for high dignitaries and selected guests. How could any of those highly respectable people be playing such an infantile trick in such a serious game? The officers proceeded with delicate tact, and finally succeeded in identifying the culprit. He was no other person than the local archbishop, who had a great fondness for the game. The large pectoral cross that rested on his chest was at the exact angle required for the troubling reflection, and its polished fine metal sent the sun's rays on their unmerciful errand with unerring accuracy. The archbishop's discomfiture and embarrassment when he had to be escorted to a distant seat, and the repressed glee of the bystanders, was a joyful event for Hardy—lovable atheist that he was, with a personal feud against God, Church, and ecclesiastical authorities. That day he enjoyed the incident more than the game itself. The sanctity of the game had been upheld. Nothing can be allowed to distract a batsman in the conscientious discharge of his duties on the field—not even the holy cross of a Church dignitary.

Sportsmen need the utmost concentration for their very existence. It is a treat in itself, and a lesson for life if one knows how to value its import and profit by its application,

to watch a golfer addressing the ball, a goalkeeper preparing himself to save a penalty kick, a tennis player tensing
himself to serve. I have noticed that tennis players, when
serving at important games, keep a spare ball in a pocket,
or if the bulging pocket turns out to be for them less
comfortable or aesthetic, in a special device attached to the
small of the back from where the ball can be retrieved by
just bringing back the hand at level height. The spare ball
is there, of course, in case the first serve fails and has to be
repeated. But why cannot they, I asked myself when I first
noticed that peculiarity, simply get another ball from the
attending ball boys, who would be only too ready and
proud to supply it immediately? The reason is that in
doing so, the player would lose concentration. To play his
first ball, he has brought into focus all his senses, limbs,
muscles, thought, and energy, and if the first shot fails
and he would have to turn to the boy for his next ball, the
spell of all that preparation would be irreparably broken
and he would have to start from scratch again with the
corresponding loss of vital energy. Rather, with the ball
securely and daintily hanging from the grip at his back, if
he fails the first service, he has only to reach gently behind
with his hand, retrieve the spare ball, and raise it into
position without any loss of concentration at the vital
instant. Concentration is precious, and nothing is to be
allowed to interfere with it. A good player nurses his
movements and prepares his emergencies to achieve a
maximum of concentration at the crucial moments of the
game. That is the secret of victory.

I know a successful businessman who rose from the
lowest rung in a factory to owner and manager of a much
larger concern in that branch of industry. I never asked
him directly what was the formula of his spectacular rise
in his field, but I observed him closely with loving interest.

At home he devoted all his attention to whatever was before him, whether it was to repair a toy for his child or discuss an outing with his wife or eat or talk. The theme of his business never once surfaced during all his hours at home. On the other hand, after he got into his car in the morning to go to the office, he changed visibly within minutes. His mind was already on his business, his face changed, he let all the details of the day's work come up in his mind, he grew silent and concentrated. Soon he was responding with pointed accuracy to all the different technical questions with which his subordinates approached him. He was a different man. His natural capacity to concentrate on the business at hand so long as required, and to drop it entirely from his mind as soon as it was over, was the trait in his character responsible for his quick and steady climb. Unusual gift of instant concentration.

The point need not be belabored. In business, in sports, in studies, in life, the power of concentration is the key to prompt, efficient, successful action. In analyzing, then, why we do not reach the levels of productivity and satisfaction we know to be within our reach, we can well examine the factors that weaken our concentration. These can be several, and often not obvious, but the most general and influential of all of them are fear and insecurity. We lose our concentration when we feel insecure. Whatever our faculties, our experience, our interest, and our determination, if at the moment of going into action we feel uneasy, unsafe, insecure, all our preparation will collapse and our performance will be far below our possibilities. Fear defeats concentration, and lack of concentration results in poor work.

Imagine a person watching an interesting movie in a comfortable cinema. Normally he would be absorbed in it, following the suspenseful plot with rapt concentration. But imagine that that person knows a band of murderers is after him and is likely to follow him into the cinema and finish him there. Will he take much notice of the film? Not likely. He will be looking back, watching every corner, and suspecting every movement, ready to make his escape immediately at the least suspicion. Even if he watches the screen, he will not follow what goes on there, and will not remain out of interest to see the end. He is totally frightened, and therefore unable to concentrate on the movie. Fear makes concentration impossible.

My students often ask me, "Why can't I concentrate?" There are many reasons and many circumstances. Each person is different, and his or her lack of attention is due in each case to a different and unique combination of individual factors. But by and large, I have reached a broad conclusion that substantially contributes to understanding many cases and even helps some. The conclusion is that the more insecure the boy or girl is, the harder he or she finds it to concentrate; and, on the contrary, the students who are more psychologically secure are those who concentrate with greater ease in studies as in everything they do. A reliable student usually has a healthy home background without traumas or problems, has a circle of friends among whom he moves freely and confidently, has regular habits and normal health. When anything in his family history or his personal experience has gone wrong and has created a ground of diffidence or a subconscious wound, he feels unsure and threatened, and his concentration is impaired. He is fidgety, jumpy, unsteady. He sits down with his books for a long spell of private study in view of the forthcoming examination. He opens one textbook as the first subject that has to be prepared, but soon he puts it aside and takes another because, after all, this other subject is more difficult and has to be tackled first. Once the chain is broken, it will be broken again. The second textbook is now set aside, and a third one taken in hand. Or maybe the first one, which is now realized to be the really important subject, is taken up again and paged through intensely . . . till it is exchanged for a different one. Nothing seems to stick in his hands, and definitely nothing sticks in his mind. His whole body bears witness to the instability of his mind. His chair dances while he changes position, leans now on one leg, now on another, turns the chair around to ride it like a horse, and back to position one to start the merry-go-round once more.

Soon his organism asks for the ritual pause. The tea break. Each room has a kerosene stove with its ceremonial pin to free the escape hole when it gets blocked, and tea powder, sugar, and milk. The ceremony takes its time, and in that precisely lies its value. The milk is boiled, the powder is added, the sugar goes with it, the mixture is stirred, the cups are filled, and the drink of the gods enjoyed in company. The company is important, as it means that the fellow student invited now to partake of the brew will, within the next hour, feel obliged to return the invitation so that another pause is assured and life with all its hardships can be faced again.

I have lived in a students' hostel for many years and I have had ample occasion to observe the varied and resourceful means by which the students manage to break the monotony of scholastic concentration. I have seen a student read one by one all the pages in a chapter of the textbook and have asked him immediately after it, "What have you read?" only to get the resigned answer, "I don't remember." Instant reading and instant forgetting. External activity without internal concentration. The result will

be printed in the final list on the public notice board at the
end of the course.

In one particular case, I was faced with a student of
obvious intelligence and refined upbringing who, nevertheless, seemed to be helplessly unable to concentrate on
any academic subject, and his studies were in serious
danger as he was not coming up to the minimum standard
required for continuation. His lack of concentration was
notorious. Even in an ordinary conversation or when
reading the newspaper or watching television he would
break off constantly to do something else and break off
again for yet something else in a flittering behavior whose
only constant factor was its lack of constancy. He was the
living image of a perpetual distraction. His own history
had something to do with it. As a very small child he had
been abandoned by his parents, rescued by a servant of
the family who took pity on him, and later accepted by a
distant relative into an already large family, where he
grew well but with the always felt, yet never expressed,
inferiority of his different origin. Complete scenario for a
permanent insecurity. The feeling was latent, of course,
and the exemplary attention he received from his new
parents made it difficult to guess that underneath there
could be such shaky foundations. But that was the case.

The fine boy was eaten up inside by his uncertain past.
The wound of the first exposure had never closed, the
anguish of passing from hand to hand had left its mark,
the friction of sharing a home as an outsider continued to
weigh on his mind, the inability to trust anybody had
imprinted itself deeply into his conscience, and the fear
that he could be abandoned again, could be betrayed by
those closest to him, could be left alone to face a hostile
world, was somberly and devastatingly at work in the
dark recesses of his sensitive soul. He was radically

insecure, and it was that insecurity that made him unable to fix his attention for long on any subject. His mind at once darted, shook, hesitated. When the feet are not steady, even the best marksman cannot take aim. The boy's feet shook, and his aim was erratic. He could not concentrate for all he was worth, and the loving advice his parents gave and the threatening scoldings his teachers subjected him to succeeded only in making him all the more shaky and uncertain. In such circumstances he could not do justice to his studies, could not use his brains nor trust his memory. He was unable to concentrate, and thus he could not use his own resources. For him, the way to an academic career lay across the recovery of his lost confidence.

A diagnosis is not a solution, but it clears the way for possible action when all concerned have the goodwill and the genuine interest to improve matters. And even more important than an academic career is to uncover the wound of insecurity and heal it. That holds good for all of us.

THE BISHOP'S LETTER

I am talking in a group, large or small, and after a certain level of mutual confidence and initial intimacy has been established, I hint at new ideas, challenge standard attitudes, outline bold paths of creative action. Then I ask the group: How do you feel? And a long silence follows. Eyes look down, feet shift, pencils dance in idle hands. Nobody speaks. I let the silence speak. It is the silence of fear. Those same people were until a moment ago taking a most active and lively part in the discussions, and the only trouble I had was to keep them in check, put order in their interventions, and see to it that the session did not degenerate into a political meeting. Each in his or her own style was contributing something to the live exchange. Ideas, arguments, objections, jokes, to keep the mind working in the noble exercise of creative thinking. But now all keep quiet. And so do I.

Ruthlessly, revengefully, pitilessly, I let the silence drag. I let them feel their own struggle. Let them sense the awkwardness of their reluctance to speak. They guess they have much to say, what has been said is important, and they know their role is to ask for clarification, to contribute parallel experiences, to challenge, to approve, to oppose. And yet now nobody stirs. The minutes pass and the silence is not broken. And the longer time passes, the harder it becomes to speak. Someone had thought of an innocent remark to make, and that would have been fine for a start, but not now after the embarrassing pause. Now something more important has to be said. And nobody says it.

I repeat my question: How do you feel? On purpose I have not asked for evaluation or criticism but for feelings. Do not tell me what you think, but tell me how you feel. It is less threatening to manifest feelings than ideas, and that can make reactions easier and more truthful. Feelings lead then up to the attitudes that cause them, and the web of the multiple analysis can be untangled in the fascinating games of the mind. But now even feelings are not forthcoming. I wait and I repeat the question. I know from past experiences the answers that are going to come. "I am confused." "I was not paying attention." "I was distracted." "I do not remember what you said." "I got lost." "I feel funny." "I am annoyed and I don't know why."

Fine. You are confused. The mind can manufacture its own smoke screen with utmost speed. It has sensed trouble. Some unfamiliar ideas are being expressed, and it will be dangerous to accept them and unpleasant to oppose them. Solution: ignore them. That is, do not see them, do not understand them, do not grasp them. Feel confused. Honestly and genuinely confused. Now the confusion does not allow you to see, and you can relax. You cannot be called to give an opinion or express a judgment. You are sincerely confused. Stay with your confusion. Fear generates the confusion, and the confusion gives you immunity. A perfect trick of the resourceful mind.

You are distracted. You were not so before. You were quite alive and alert and enjoying everything with instant attention. Don't tell me that, of course, it was so all along, but now, precisely because of that unremitting attention, you are beginning to feel tired and this explains the distraction. Maybe, but it does not explain why the distraction should begin exactly here. Some challenging ideas have begun to be expressed, and you have got distracted on cue. What was prompting the distraction inside you? Your own fear complex. Do not disturb me. Do not rock the boat. Do not get me into trouble. Do not make me say yes or no to something that makes me feel uncomfortable both ways. Do not corner me. All right. But notice that your timely distraction is only your neat escape. You do not want to be questioned, do not want to be challenged, do not want to be made to think. You do not want even the thought to remain in your mind, where it may surface again in your solitude and disturb you again, and so you get distracted. Not that you plan to get distracted or that you do it consciously by an act of your will; I know it is not that way. It is your subconscious that comes to your rescue and makes you innocently and totally distracted so that the thought is not inscribed in your mind at all, and you can claim the total immunity of your true ignorance before the group and before your own conscience. Perfect defense.

You do not remember. Curious, isn't it? You heard it, you understood it, you followed it, and now that you are asked to think about it and give your reaction, you cannot recall it. Blank. Someone has wiped clean the files in your memory, and your very recent memory at that. People do not easily admit to a lack of intelligence, yet they will readily admit a lack of memory. You do not remember, and you cannot be blamed for it. You would be happy to contribute your comments if only you could remember what we are talking about; but it just has escaped your mind and there is nothing that can be done about it. You do not want, of course, to inconvenience the group by having the whole matter repeated only for your benefit. No, no, that would be unfair, and you cannot allow it. Let the discussion proceed. That is, let the silence proceed. Nobody wants to take the plunge, and one excuse follows another. One way or another, this is certainly a learning session.

I take a look at the faces around me. Some are tense, some are blankly relaxed. The image surges in my mind of an impregnable fortress without a gap in the solid rampart. No way to get through. If an army would come out to fight, we could engage in battle; but as it is, the field is empty under the vertical walls. No champions to fight their cause. Not that there are no ideas, opinions, suggestions, objections. Rather, the fear that has gripped the mind does not allow them to come out and show themselves. That is what the empty faces and bland smiles mean. The most intelligent audience can lose its response if the invisible veil of fear descends upon the meeting. *Fear inhibits thinking.*

And then come the private excuses. Some people feel the need of justifying their silence after the public ordeal is over, and they volunteer plausible explanations. "I did not speak in the group to give a chance to others whose need was greater." There are some truly thoughtful persons who keep quiet so that others may speak, and that can be a very sensitive contribution to a common discussion. But there is also the possibility that the supposed kindness is just a ruse to avoid trouble. Let the others speak so that you may not have to open your mouth. Perfect safety. Or again: "I did not come in because I realized the meeting was getting too long and you were tired." How can I not thank such a considerate person? And yet his or her consideration may only be a screen for his or her shyness. Yes, I was tired. But it was for me to call the end of the session, not for anyone else. The remark is similar to one I have frequently found in letters: "I know that you are a busy person, so you need not answer this letter." Very kind of you. But you have said a few things in that letter which I very much want to answer, and in a way which you may not like, and so it may very well be that, when you tell me that I need not answer your letter, what you really mean is that you do not want me to answer it because you are afraid of my answer. When people write a letter, they usually want an answer. Your generosity in waiving your right to an answer sounds to me as if you fear to be told what you do not want to hear. You have expressed your own opinions in your letter, and do not want to see them contradicted. I am jolly well going to answer your letter, whether you like it or not. I am the guardian of my time and I know what to do with it. And I like to answer the letters I get.

Once I got a letter from a bishop to whom I had sent a book of mine. As I knew him and knew also his interest in modern books, I valued his opinion, which I solicited in a friendly covering letter. He answered promptly, and this was the answer: "Kindly accept my thanks for the book you have sent me and my congratulations for having written it. Some people will say that you have said too much in it, while others will think that you have said too little, which may mean after all that you have said what should be said. I am surely looking forward to reading it as soon as I find the time. Meanwhile rest assured of . . ." and so forth. For a moment I wondered whether it was a printed form the busy bishop had ready for such occasions and he had just signed a copy and mailed it to me. It could apply to any book by any author any time. It was a perfect specimen of formal style. It said nothing at all. Or rather, it said just one thing, and that very clearly: that he did not want to say anything. I had a profound suspicion that he had in fact read the book, did not want to commit himself about it, and so wrote the safe letter at once as though he were still "looking forward" to reading the book. A clever maneuver. A letter written before reading the book was only an acknowledgment of receipt, and on the other hand, it exempted him from writing again and having to say something about the book. Or maybe he did just what he said, that is, he wrote at once before reading the book to be in the clear with me, and he is still looking forward to reading the book. I shall never know. The little incident impressed me deeply because I had known the man before and I had expected a better reaction. I was sadly disappointed.

Desire for safety impairs our powers of reasoning. Thinking is the most dangerous activity on earth, and we instinctively know that. This explains the meager use we make of our most exalted faculty. As a teacher of mathematics, I have often wondered why the subject enjoys such low popularity ratings and is considered so hard and exclusive. When the question comes up, we are wont to mention indulgently that math requires brains; but that is only a way of pushing ourselves forward. The fact is that some students with obvious brains do badly at math while others who score high in mathematics do poorly in almost everything else. Psychologists say something that, again with some reservations, throws unexpected light on the matter. They say people are afraid of mathematics because they are afraid of rigor, logic, and exactness. We do not like to see things too clearly, to be forced to admit conclusions, to have to conform to exacting standards. Life does not make much sense, and we feel comfortable in its loose, informal, hazy atmosphere of familiar customs without going very deep into why we do this and why we think this way. Clear-cut definitions scare us. And mathematics, with its relentless quest for the exact answer and the flawless proof, does not quite fit into our casual way of living. In any case, here again, it is fear that precludes understanding. Let this be a consolation for whoever has suffered at school with mathematics. And a lesson to all to still our fears if we want our brains to work.

A HOSPITAL NIGHT

Fear of loneliness is essentially fear of meeting oneself. When an old person fears to be left alone, it is not that he is afraid of darkness or ghosts or of falling or being robbed. Or maybe it is all that and many more such things together on the surface of his mind, but deep within his heart, what is making him uneasy and begging for company is the fear of having to face himself. A companion is fundamentally a distraction. There is talk, smiles, looking at each other, sensing a presence, knowing that someone is by the side, and thus being happily freed from the threat of having to think about oneself. If there are several persons around, so much the better. The talking is louder and the topics wider, and the danger of having to converge on oneself recedes even further. But then the people begin to leave one by one. Each departure brings closer the moment of truth. For all their goodwill, they cannot remain forever. Their kindness delays their going, and with the last one to go lingers in merciful errand the inevitable moment. Then he goes. And all is dark. The lonely man can take refuge in a book or in the TV set, but he knows all too well that such a stratagem is only begging time. The showdown is unavoidable. Voices fall silent, images fade, and he remains alone with himself. Dreadful moment.

The man has his whole life behind him. That life

means memories and incidents and stories to be told to others when conversation is on, and that is fine. But that whole life also means personal, intimate memories which are not for telling, and above all, that past life means a set of values, of attitudes, of options taken and positions defended which seemed to be the true positions at the time, but it is very doubtful whether they retain their validity anymore. Points of view have changed, and what looked praiseworthy at the time looks contemptible now, and actions of which he was proud then could not bear retelling now. He is afraid of questioning his own past, of weighing anew his decisions and evaluating his life. He cannot bear the thought that it might turn out to have been empty when it is already too late to do anything about it now. He wants to avoid by all means that inquisitive look on his past, and that is why he wants to avoid the solitude that may inexorably lead him to the dreaded self-examination.

This situation is particularly clear in the case of an old person, and that is why I have taken that example first; but with due adjustments in time and character, the same analysis holds good for any person of any age before the test of solitude. Moments of solitude are moments of self-judgment for all, and that gives solitude its pallor. An enterprising young man is in the midst of an active campaign for a noble cause with wide publicity, a large following, and dedicated enthusiasm in hard work and self-sacrificing energy. He is genuinely busy with his complex work and has no time to rest. No time to think. No time to be all by himself. He is never alone. He cannot afford to be. By this I do not mean that he is so busy that he always needs to have some of his coworkers near him and therefore he cannot be alone; what I mean is that he cannot afford to be alone because if he takes time out, sits quietly by himself and thinks, he may see the futility of all he is doing and may drop the whole work. That is why he cannot afford solitude. And that is why he dreads it.

He says he is by nature sociable, gregarious, an extrovert, and therefore always has to be surrounded by people. The fact is that he is afraid, insecure, inwardly suspecting that all that impressive work he is carrying out, though outwardly praiseworthy, socially oriented, and popularly appreciated, is in fact the result of his own thirst for power, his ambition, and his pride. If he withdraws for a while and looks at himself in the mirror of his conscience, he is going to find that out at once, and therefore he cannot afford the mirror and the withdrawal.

He says he is afraid of loneliness. What he is afraid of is truth. The home truth that not all he is doing is so wonderful and altruistic as it appears to be. To be alone invites reflection, and reflection can be hard. Better not to know. Better not to have to think. Let people surround me so that I may not have the chance to turn my attention on myself, and may go on without a hindrance.

Fear of solitude is also fear of boredom. We may be good at entertaining others, but we are not so good at entertaining ourselves. Being with others is a welcome distraction; being alone is a trying monologue. What we call boredom is incapacity to be with ourselves. We know how limited our resources are, and fear to be left alone with them. We have heard our own jokes and we know our own stories, and we have made other people laugh with them, but we are not likely to laugh at them by ourselves. Again, there is not much in our life that is interesting and amusing, and we do not like to be reminded of it. To be bored is, in a way, to acknowledge our little worth (a wise man used to say that only the fool gets bored), and to avoid the verdict, we avoid the occasion.

Modern men and women will do anything not to feel alone. They will watch TV, keep the radio on, hold a newspaper in their hands even if they do not read it—just as they were not listening to the radio or seeing the screen. The physical touch, the noise, the changing colors on the screen, create the impression of company, and they beat solitude by drugging the senses. People feel lonely even— maybe especially—in the midst of a crowd, and that is why we've had to invent a device to go with us and play music in our ears while we walk the street. We don't like to feel lonely. And so we don earphones in the crowded city. Fill my ears with sound if you cannot fill my soul with confidence. Not all who listen to music do so out of love of music. Not all who clap their hands and cheer in unison at an open-air concert do so out of enthusiasm for the performance; many do it out of the need to belong to a group, to defeat solitude, to feel brotherhood with a waving and swinging crowd that creates for a while the boisterous illusion that they are not alone. The real per- formers at such happenings are not the singers on the stage but the audience on the grounds. And their real need is not to enjoy art but to fight loneliness. Noise to scare away ghosts.

I know a young woman who, influenced by some ascetical writings, decided she would keep total silence on Sundays. Such practice is not uncommon in India, but it was unusual in a young girl of lively disposition. She announced her resolution to family and friends; she would lead a normal life on Sundays at home, even go anywhere and do anything, but she would not utter a word. I made it a point to visit her home every Sunday to tease her with my presence, defenseless as she was in her charmingly indignant silence, and watched for the coming events. They were not late in coming. The first Sunday she had a headache. The next she remained the whole day in her room. She held on for a few more Sundays, always making up on Monday for the words lost on Sunday, and soon she was back to normal and the experiment was forgotten. Her attempt at heroics was short-lived.

To refrain from speaking for twenty-four hours is not a great feat by itself. But the mental isolation such a silence signifies and effects can become unbearable for an active mind. To be silent while others talk is obvious strain, and to withdraw into solitude to avoid the talking company is to invite trouble with one's own thoughts. The burden of silence is not so much the discipline of holding one's tongue as the awkwardness of meeting one's thoughts. Man afraid of his own shadow.

Spiritual masters point out that even in prayer we tend to talk too much and prefer activity to silence. Jesus already remarked on it in the Sermon on the Mount, and the tendency continues. Again here, we talk too much so that we may not have to listen; in this case, listen to God, who speaks through our conscience. Drown the inner voice with outside recitations, and fill the silence with discourses of the mind. No chance to listen, no chance to see, no simplicity to stand open before God and face his presence. We want the security of our thoughts, however shaky they may be, rather than the unfamiliar challenge of the unknown demand. We talk ourselves out of our own capacity to reflect. We avoid solitude, even in prayer, to avoid judgment.

After visiting a friend in the hospital, I stood up and held his hand while he lay in bed at the end of a long day. He clasped my hand and would not loosen his grip, warm with the fever of his malaise and wet with perspiration. I sensed, through the telling language of the mute gesture, the poignancy of the moment for the sick man who was

saying good-bye to the last visitor of the day before
settling down to another long and lonely night. It was not
physical pain, not danger, not fever, that held his mind in
terror, but the dark fear of one more night with himself
alone in a hospital room. He was an active man who fell
asleep daily as soon as his head hit the pillow after a day
packed with unceasing activity. And now the day had
been idle, and the night loomed ahead in unwonted
sleeplessness through unfriendly hours. How could he
live in the white solitude of his aseptic bed sheets? A
strong man afraid to face his weakness. Still holding my
hand, he murmured, almost to himself, "Don't go. I'm
afraid." Momentary breakdown before the onslaught of
loneliness. He would have to be himself, and himself
alone, through the sleepless night. His grip on my hand
loosened up slowly, and he looked away. Alone through
the hospital night. Is not the whole life a hospital night?

THE SUPREME GUEST

The shadow of insecurity has followed humanity since birth in relentless reminder of our mortal condition, and now it lengthens as winter approaches and a silent chill settles on the landscape of life and on the human heart. Like the last snow that will not melt or leaves that fall and will not green again. The last flight of migratory birds that has left and we shall not see next year. The slow farewell that nature autographs on our earthly horizon with the artistic sadness of a last flourish. Signs of the last departure, and with them the final insecurity of the last exit from the stage. We are going and we do not know where. The uncertainty of the first birth reflected in the uncertainty of the last one, like parallels that encompass man's life on earth with symmetrical finality. Death is a new birth, and carries with it all the memories, the trauma, the anxiety, of the first one. The original memory has been projected across the span of life, touching every instant and coloring every event, and now marks the point of departure with the same definitiveness with which it marked the point of entry. Last uncertainty in the long series of unknowns. The gate of death at the end of the road of life. And the last courage to walk through it.

Death is a departure. A departure leaves something and opens up to something else. Parting is always painful, and therefore death, signified and prepared by all the partial departures through life, brings pain in its final farewell from all we know. Every journey prepares for death. Every farewell is an anointing. Every airport or railway station is an anteroom of the cemetery, not for its bombs and accidents but for the separation it brings about among us and the people who know us. The awkwardness of the situation, the impossibility of finding any sensible thing to say, the annoyance when the departure is delayed, not because we shall arrive later but because we are stuck with our well-wishers for an extra period without relief. We urge them to leave us and go back; they insist in fulfilling to the end their duty of seeing us safely off, and the polite agony continues on both sides. Finally the separation, the last kiss, tender with the desire not to leave love unsaid and restrained before the profane presence of the milling crowd; and then the first instant of solitude, the dark veil, the somber mood, the reluctant heart, the defeated mind, and the body that walks mechanically along prisonlike corridors and through narrow doors into the unknown.

We have practiced death many times in our lives. Every time we get a little closer to reality. Every farewell is charged with greater urgency as we unconsciously measure its proximity to the last one to come. And yet parting does not become easier with practice; it becomes harder. And the last parting is the hardest of all. It is parting from everything and everybody and forever. That is the hard part of dying.

Kalelkar says in his book *Death, the Closest Friend*: "Death is painful because it involves separation; but of itself it is not fearful. The fear part of death has been added by man." The fear comes from the other face of death, the one that looks ahead. Death is departure from the known and entrance into the unknown. And man fears the unknown. The eternal hang-up on security. For all the fervor of faith, the conviction of reason, the educated instinct, and the vehement desire, the dark beyond remains uncertain, and that supreme uncertainty induces fear in the heart of man. Fear of death is in fact the basic fear that is reflected in all other fears through life, the sum total of all partial fears, the root from where all fears derive. Fear of sickness is fear of death, fear of a storm is fear of death, fear of loneliness is fear of death. We fear that which can hurt us, and every hurt is a diminution of vitality, a loss of blood, a foretaste of death. Thus death is present in all our fears, and our last day is anticipated in the image of all other days.

Death is an encounter with the unknown, and therefore we fear the encounter. To make it worse, the encounter is sudden and we are always taken by surprise, which increases the trepidation when we think of it. We know, of course, that death is coming, and sometimes doctors even give us a time limit and we know we cannot last; but we are never prepared for the announced meeting. The Bible calls death a thief. A thief comes when we least expect him and takes away something precious from us. We all fear thieves.

In India death is called a "guest," and there is some interesting thinking behind that. The Indian word for guest is *atithi*, literally "the one without a date." The true guest is the one who comes unannounced. No phone call and no postcard with the date and time of the proposed arrival. He just knocks at the door, and when they open from inside, there he is, smiling with his luggage at his feet and maybe his wife and a couple of children by his side to make up the scene. Total surprise. And the gracious host opens wide the door, welcomes all to his home, and does not ask how many days the sojourn will last. If there is no date in coming, there is no date in going. Let the uncertainty be complete.

Death is the Perfect Guest *(Param Atithi)*. No date, no hour, no notice. A knock at the door. A gaunt skeleton with a sickle and an hourglass and a winning smile, as far as a skeleton can manage a smile, is standing on the doorstep. We ask him in at once. The welcome mat for the unannounced guest. We bid him sit down and make himself at home while we get ready to accompany him. We know his errand and will not keep him waiting as he has other similar business to attend to. What with the population increase and the escalation of violence, it is a busy time for him. There we go now, cheerfully hand in hand and waving good-bye. He knows the way.

This idea of death as a guest is the conceptual foundation for the famed Oriental hospitality where every door is open and every guest welcome, and even an enemy will be given shelter in one's tent and will be safe and honored there for the length of his stay. Death is a guest, and it prepares its coming by sending messengers during our life to test our readiness and train our responses. Every guest is an image, every knock a reminder. These reminders are not meant to frighten us, but on the contrary, to do away with our fears by teaching us to welcome with joyful eagerness the unexpected and the unknown. Hospitality is an education for the host. The open door, the ready smile, the bountiful banquet. The arrival of a guest is not an occasion for mourning but for rejoicing. The guest is friendly, there are family ties in between, we like to chat together, to eat together, to show our guest the sights of the town, to renew the kinship, to strengthen the relationship. There may be a little inconvenience in making satisfactory arrangements for our guest, preparing the room, cleaning the house, upgrading the menus, adjusting timetables, but the joy of welcoming a sincere friend in our home offsets the small trouble of the added labor. A family visit is a date of joy.

Death is a family visit. By meeting the messengers, we have come to know the Master. Familiarity has been established and misgivings have been proved baseless. A knock at the door does not frighten us anymore. We open the door with confidence, with happiness, with the eager anticipation of a pleasant visit from a beloved relative. The last surprise will not be a surprise anymore. We have so often thought of him when opening the door that when he finally appears, it will be a longed-for meeting, an expected revelation. A long life of generous hospitality is the best preparation for a placid and pleasant death. A family reunion. Welcome to the Supreme Guest.

I know the blessings of Indian hospitality, and for some years I literally lived on it. I knocked at the doors of families I did not know, shared their meals in the day and their floor at night, and moved after a few days to another house in the neighborhood, often running the length of a street in a festival of acquaintances inconceivable in other lands. Sometimes I had difficulty finding a house, but I never had to interrupt my urban pilgrimage for lack of a host. Once I returned rather late at night to the house where I was lodging for the week. I still had a couple of days to be in that house and then I would think of the next one, but till then I could stay safely in that house. Or so I thought.

On arrival one night, I met a situation I had come to recognize. The woman in the house had entered her recurring days of ritual impurity, and therefore could not cook, wash, or clean the house for that time, which meant in practice for me that I should take leave promptly not to create more problems for them. They also understood and

were relieved, in their helplessness, to see me depart
gratefully on my own while the woman sat in a corner, her
hair hanging loose as warning sign of her monthly holiday
from housework.

It was late and dark in the sultry night. What door to
knock at, this time? A thought came to me. A few days
before, while going to work on my bicycle, a young man
on his own bike had pushed alongside and, while we
cycled together, had introduced himself as a reader of my
books, though he had never met me, and on knowing of
my itinerant life from house to house, had offered his own
and mentioned the address. It was close by, and I went
there. There was still light inside. I knocked, and to my
relief, the young man himself opened the door. I explained
my need, and he acted at once. His parents had already
gone to sleep, and he was spreading his own mat for the
night; so he signaled to me to lie down on the mat he had
prepared for himself while he took another corner and
wished me good night. In the morning he would inform
his parents that they had a guest with them since the
previous night. I lay down relieved, thinking, while sleep
came, where else could such practical hospitality be practiced with such ease? It was a pleasure to meet the boy's
parents next morning, and once again to go to work with
him alongside. I wondered whether, by welcoming me
with such spontaneous grace, they were consciously prac-
ticing the last encounter with the Supreme Guest, but at
any rate, the attitude was in their culture and they had
acted in perfect consonance with their tradition. In so
doing, they had solved my problem for that time.

This latent attitude may be a partial explanation of a
phenomenon I have observed repeatedly in India: people
here die with greater naturalness than in the West. There
is less anxiety, less worry, less fuss, about the fact of

death. Yes, the time comes and we go, and there is no need to broadcast the event. Literally and healthily, let me die in peace. A friend of mine with a sense of humor says that in India, when visiting a terminally ill patient, one greets him cheerfully and says, "Congratulations! I hear you are breathing your last. Isn't it great!" This may be a little exaggerated, but it makes the point. We live here closer to earth, open to nature, steeped in faith, and ready to receive the last visit of the Secret Guest who under so many disguises has been visiting us all along in this earthly life. Spiritual traditions have very practical consequences.

Karsandas Manek, poet and mystic, has a poem on death as the surprise visit of God's messenger. I liked the poem, mentioned that to him, and he told me with the impish smile that went with his always lively conversation, "I am going to tell you why you like it. The poem is true. People think that we poets just imagine things and situations and then describe as real what we have imagined. Such was not the case with this poem. One day I felt acutely sick and called at once a doctor who was also a friend. He told me, 'That was a heart attack, and you know what that means. Get ready for the trip, because the next one may be the last.' He was a good friend and a good doctor, and I believed the diagnosis and appreciated the frankness. But if he was a doctor, I am a poet, and that very moment, under the heart attack and with the feelings that the news had aroused in me, I took the pen and wrote that poem at one stroke. It is not an imagined situation, but an actual experience. That is why you, without knowing it, have liked it." This is the poem in translation:

> God's messenger has shown in light,
> an urgent message on his lips:

Roll up your tent, you pilgrim soul,
and leave the lush and fragrant fields!

Welcome to you, God's messenger!
Welcome to your commanding writ!
My pilgrimage is now completed,
I leave the lush and fragrant fields.

No testament for me to write,
no last desires to express;
no wisdom words for me to utter,
no lost occasions to regret.

Nothing is hidden in my life,
no double dealings in my word;
I lived expecting you at each moment.
Come, take me to the house of God!

POET AND PAINTER

Here is another poem by my poet friend. However much it pales in translation, it was written also while the aftereffects of the heart attack were still with him:

I saw life for the first time
when I listened to death's chime
    at my door.

What was a tangled quiz of pain and pleasure
made sense in sudden shape as priceless treasure
    for the first time.

The devious ways of the affairs of man
became straight lines in God's eternal plan
    for the first time.

The prison walls of this ungainly world
shone brightly with the dazzling glint of gold
    for the first time.

I saw my way, I found my place at last
when death revealed my future and my past
    for the first time.

It is a little late to find out about ourselves, but better late than never. And if we can anticipate a glimpse of that posthumous light to our present situation, we can gain balance and courage to go on with the puzzle while we are at it. The healthy consciousness that this is not going to last brings a sense of proportion to everything we do or experience, big or small, pleasant or painful. The picture of life is cut down to size inside the frame of death. Death can help us to make the best of each chance instead of frightening us into inaction. Death's role in life is to give perspective.

An intelligently written suspense novel makes sense suddenly and explosively when we reach the last page, and never before. The involved plot, the shady characters, the improbable culprit, the discarded hypotheses, the misleading hints, the hopeless tangle—all suddenly become clear and evident when after a laborious reading we turn to the last page and learn the last clue to the tense intrigue. It was obvious, of course! We suspected it all the time. Who else could it be? Now it is clear why he said that and what his true intentions were. Even that small detail that had seemed irrelevant, though it left in our minds the suspicion that if it had been explicitly mentioned, there must have been a reason for it, shows now its meaning and the importance of a small point in unraveling a big plot. Everything becomes transparent, and the novel is remembered as a masterful intrigue.

Something of this happens with life. After all, mystery novels thrive because life is a mystery. On the last page events of the past that seemed unconnected and meaningless suddenly become intelligible and important, forming part of a harmonic whole. An incomplete event is essentially unintelligible, and life is very much incomplete as we get up every morning to face a new day with all its question marks hiding away from our view. An unfinished poem, an interrupted building, a half-drafted speech, an incomplete picture. We miss the whole and cannot make sense of it. Let the last touch come, the last word, the last brush, and the picture will emerge in fullness of meaning and beauty.

Once an amateur painter of some repute volunteered to do my portrait. I was flattered and submitted to the necessary torture of sitting for hours with as little movement as possible. Humble sacrifice for art's sake. After the first session, when I had sat through the limits of my endurance and she seemed to have done quite a bit of daubing on the canvas, I got up and went good-naturedly to inspect the initial sketch, ready to praise it no matter what it would look like. But she stopped me sharply, covered the canvas with a cloth, and told me with a smile that only served to emphasize how serious she was in her prohibition, "You will see your portrait when it is finished; if you see it halfway, you are not going to like it." What she said made me think. If I see my portrait halfway, I am not going to like it. A few uncertain lines, patches of color, lifeless expression. On the whole, not worthy to be called a human face, much less mine. A caricature at most, a good wish in color, a painted prophecy, but in itself, nothing to look at for now. Wait and see. In due time you will be shown the finished work, and then you will recognize yourself in it. Look at the portrait only when it is finished.

I understood the artist's injunction and obeyed it. By then another thought was in my mind. Do not criticize your life while it is halfway. You may not like it, you may not understand it, you may not be able to make sense of a few stray lines and a few haphazard colors. Whose portrait is this? Nothing to look at. Just a way of spoiling a piece of canvas and a good deal of time. Most people complain that life does not make sense. Wait a little. The portrait is still incomplete. There are still more sessions to come. Have a little patience. Those lines and colors are still to acquire firmness and definiteness. The whole face is still to emerge, the eyes are to be focused, the smile has to be lit, the whole expression has to come alive for that face to be yours and for you to recognize it and accept it. Wait till the portrait is finished, and then you will appreciate the work and thank the painter. The completed result will justify all the impatience about the long delay.

This is the meaning of painter and poet. We understand life when we welcome death. This is not the medieval hobby of keeping a skull handy on one's table to be reminded in the midst of any enjoyment of the transitoriness of all earthly pleasures. That is a fairly morbid fashion, likely to become a killjoy for life. The point is rather to gain perspective by integrating death in our thought, taming its fears, and softening its impact.

Our way of speaking is witness to our reluctance to think of death. We speak of what will happen "when he is no more," of her "passing away," of his "will," which, of course, does not mean his willpower but his last will, with the "last" removed out of delicate considerateness. We eliminate words of death from our vocabulary as we eliminate ideas of death from our mind. It is not polite to call things by their names. There are taboo words that have to be replaced by euphemisms in social conversation. Fear of death is translated into fear of uttering words meaning death. This verbal and mental isolation from the one clear and definite reality of our lives can only do us harm and impair our human development.

The analogy of the portrait may have given a wrong impression, which I want to correct. It is not that we have to wait in time for the last day of our lives to understand the first. In a deeper way, our life is incomplete always, even on its last day, and is complete always at each moment that we may look at it. In fact, I must confess that when my portrait was finally completed and I was allowed to look at it, I did not like it. They say that a person never likes his own portrait, which may mean that secretly he believes he is better looking than the canvas, and in fact, when I found myself looking at the masterpiece under the beaming smile of the artist in search of praise for her work, I found it difficult to manage a smile and stutter an appreciation. My first instinct on seeing the face had been to ask, "Is that my picture?" But I realized that such reaction might sound offensive, and I stopped in time the tactless remark and contemplated wistfully my flat like-ness until I could think of something better to say and get over the crisis. The point is to bring the wisdom that the end will bring to the present moment as we live it, to remove the sting of suffering by realizing that it cannot last forever, and calm down the thrill of enthusiasm by re-minding ourselves that the high tide will turn as surely as the low. Death reveals past and future, says the poet, and that is the best help to living the present. Instead of putting aside the thought of death as something unpleas-ant and impolite, we would be better advised to invite it to our consideration and welcome it to our memory as a living part of our present moment. The fear of death deprives us of its company through life, and we are the losers.

A young boy from a Brahman family in the South Indian village of Tiruvannamalai had an unusual experience that changed his life and later, through him, the lives of many. He was sitting alone in a room in his uncle's house when he felt a sudden fear of death. Instead of resisting the fear, he acted it out. He lay down on the floor, became motionless, closed his lips tightly, and held his breath.

The thought flashed through his mind that though his body was dead, there was something in him that survived bodily death. With that experience, his fear of death vanished once and for all. That was his education. He went to live in a temple and then in a cave and then at the foot of a mountain, where he remained for life, spoke little and wrote less, and was a true source of inspiration to devoted seekers from all over the world. His angelic smile, preserved in naive photographs, is graphic witness to the peace of mind he had attained and had spread around in a message of fondness for life. Death had been his teacher.

YOUR CAPTAIN SPEAKING

It was the year of the Munich Olympics. A terrorist attack on one of the teams had stained with blood the sacred grounds of international competition, and the flags of nations had flown half-staff in stunned sorrow for athletic lives felled in youth before a watching world. The Indian hockey team had taken part in the games, and was now returning home via Rome in an Air India jumbo jet. I boarded that flight in Rome to come back to India. The huge plane had ponderously made its way to the end of the runway, had turned its nose to the tapering perspective of the long tarmac, and the four engines were straining at the leash to start their race into the sky. Inside the plane, we had adjusted our seats, fastened our seat belts, and were bracing ourselves for the immediate takeoff. We were expecting the last announcement by the routine voice of the flight attendant when suddenly we heard another voice on the internal address system. It was cold, masculine, businesslike. It said calmly and firmly, "This is your captain speaking. You are all requested to deplane immediately. I repeat. You are all requested to deplane immediately. There is a bomb scare." There was no panic, but in a matter of seconds the huge plane was empty, and it was left at the end of the runway, stately and haughty like a bird of ill omen, while we were speedily taken back to the safety of the terminal building.

There had been an anonymous phone call, we learned, to warn that a bomb had been planted in the aircraft. In view of the recent tragedy and of the fact that an Olympic team was traveling with us, the threat assumed ready credibility, and people were quick to weave theories that would explain the uncomfortable presence of a bomb somewhere in the complex body of the immense plane. I could have enjoyed the different hypotheses, much as the conjectures to solve the plot in a mystery novel, but the nagging reminder that this was not a novel I was reading but a plane I was going to be sitting in for an eight-hour journey at an altitude of several thousand feet somehow threw a pall over the proceedings and prevented me from looking at the situation with a gleeful eye.

For five hours we were kept in the waiting hall, fed intermittently by goodwill sandwiches proferred with abundant smiles and no explanations as to what was happening and what kind of future we should prepare our souls for. Police dogs, explosives experts, airline personnel came and went, and not a clue on their faces. Finally our flight was called again, and we filed eagerly into buses to identify our luggage and climb again the fateful steps onto the waiting aircraft.

It was nice to fit into the old seat again, and as mine was next to the aisle, I innocently engaged the flight attendant in a bit of small talk. After a few pleasantries I asked straight, "Has the bomb been found?" He said, "No." And there was disappointment in his voice. "We've searched every corner and the dogs have sniffed every fold and nook, but nothing has been found. The treasure hunt has proved ineffective." He managed to smile, and then added hopefully, "Most of these anonymous calls are empty threats, you know. We have to act, of course, as we have done, but then there is nothing and we proceed.

We'll soon know," he added, trying his sense of humor on me. I am the last man to fail to profit by some humor of whatever kind, but I found this joke rather out of place, and only took occasion of it to ask my next question. This was now black humor on my part, but I asked with seeming unconcern as though I were merely gathering data for an encyclopedia, "And how do these airborne bombs work; could you explain that to me?" He was too caught by now and had to supply the information with what I judged to be some reluctancy on his part. "These bombs are of two kinds," he said as though delivering a lecture to eager candidates for terrorists. "One is a time bomb, and the other an altitude bomb. The time bomb has a built-in clock in which a time is set as on an alarm clock, and when the hands get there, the contact triggers the explosive and it does its work. In the altitude bomb, the trigger is an altimeter, which measures the height at which the aircraft is flying and invites the explosion at the preset altitude. In both cases the effect is the same for practical purposes." I could see what he meant and told him so with my thanks for his helpful information. Now I knew from a competent and reliable source the two ways in which I could meet the experience. I surmised that, given the delay the flight was already under, a time bomb would have exploded already, so my bet was clearly for the altitude type. I would have to watch how high we were getting.

All this discussion had been conducted on a purely academic level. There was no anxiety, no nerves, no rush to draw up a last will before it would be too late. Each one kept one's own feelings, and politeness and graceful manners ruled all the exchanges. But then the plane started. The deafening groan, the racing windows, the receding lights, then the sudden bump, the raised angle, the calculated curve, and the lights of Rome far below in twinkling farewell. Then I was alone for a moment with my thoughts and my feelings and the shadow of the altitude bomb. Something pulled at my heart. For the first time in my life I saw death as a concrete possibility within the next few minutes. The plane was climbing steadily; the efficient altimeter could be measuring feet with relentless accuracy. Any moment now. A wild explosion, the broken body of the helpless plane, the momentary confusion, the sudden plunge, and the unannounced encounter with Italian soil. All that was for me, at that moment, not the remote statistical possibility of one chance in thousands but the very real and highly probable occurrence that might be a fact the next minute. I could do nothing but watch my feelings. I did so, and this is what I found, set down here with the same sincerity with which I experienced it in the face of death.

I was not afraid, I was angry. I know well that anger can be a cover for fear, and that may have been the case at that moment with me, but the clear feeling was anger, not fear. I was not afraid of physical pain, of the anguish of the crash, and be this a good or a bad sign, I was not afraid of meeting God and being given peremptory directives as to where to proceed. I was not shivering or out of breath or anxious, and in a way, I was surprised at not feeling disturbed by thoughts I had been led to believe would disturb me in my last earthly moments. But I was definitely angry, very angry, revolutionarily and indignantly angry, and the flush of anger surged through my being in those intense minutes. Why should I die? I was enjoying life, I was having a good time; I was doing good work; I was not old; I still had a number of books to write (strangely curious how my reluctance to die came largely out of the fact that I had not yet expressed in writing all the ideas I thought I should express); I had my old mother, who needed my visits and who should be spared the pain of seeing me die before her; I was healthy and strong, and it would be absolutely unfair to cut my life short at that moment without any fault of mine, simply for the questionable intervention of an unknown terrorist. It just was not fair, and every cell in me protested with one voice at that moment against the death sentence about to be executed.

I did not see my whole life in a flash, as I had read was one of the expected features of a predemise program. I did not experience contrition for my sins, I did not (O shame!) think of my close friends to send them a last mental message as I had always promised myself I would do to satisfy my affection and prove my fidelity. Much less did I think of the Hindu recommendation to invite kind thoughts at the last moment in the belief that the last thought in this life determines the role one is to assume in the next. Nothing of the kind. My last thought was a strong official protest that my lease was to be so abruptly terminated without previous notice and against my will. If that was going to fix my itinerary in the next world, I would have landed as a permanent member of the opposition. The anger subsided as the plane continued to climb and no loud report was heard. Maybe the altimeter was not functioning after all.

Airline personnel seem to have regular experience with such situations, because they proceeded to do a very clever thing. They started at once showing the in-flight movie they were supposed to show later. It was a fine movie, *Mary, Queen of Scots*. Hardly had it begun when I became totally engrossed in it, and only a side thought amused me for an instant, making me realize how flimsy all my preparation-for-death-as-the-moment-on-which-eternity-hangs stuff was when a simple movie was enough to make me forget in a matter of minutes all the intense experience of having faced death in the skies. I was safe for the rest of the journey. Mary, Queen of Scots, was not so fortunate.

CONDOLENCE SPEECH

One day I had been asked to visit a house where someone had died. Not a pleasant errand by any means. I did not even know the deceased and had never been to that house, but a friend of mine, who was related to the family and was concerned at the severe depression that had come upon them, urged me to visit them in their sorrow and bring some consolation to their troubled hearts. When I agreed to go, the only thing I made clear to myself was that I would not have recourse to any of the trite expressions of condolence in the catalog of standard phrases for such occasions. I would not be official, I would not feign feelings, I would not use clichés. It was a tough resolution, but I was determined to stick to it. It is very easy to repeat the expected sentence with the right intonation while stooped over and looking at the floor, waiting in silence for the whispered answer from the same catalog of stock expressions for the occasion. But I was not going to that house to do that. I put behind me all preconceived ideas and cleared my mind to react anew to the situation as it would arise.

I was ushered into a large hall with, perhaps, thirty persons in it. I walked through them, declining introductions. I knew nobody, and a few hurried introductions were going to make no difference. Death, which had taken one of them and would take us one by one on our day, was enough bond to experience closeness in that family meeting. I sat down and surveyed the white audience. In India, white is the color of mourning, and all men and women in that gathering were dressed in glaring white. So was I. I knew the rubric and had obeyed it. I saw the faces, drawn, expressionless, marked with recent tears. I let silence reign undisturbed in the whole house. It looked so fitting that for a while I thought I would not speak, and nobody indeed was asking me to do so. Our mutual presences were speaking to one another, and we knew, by sitting together, that we were doing all we could do to honor the mystery of death that had brought us together. The long silence continued without any sign of impatience from any corner. We were at ease in the shared sorrow.

Then, as I had been inwardly prompted to keep quiet, I was prompted to speak. By then I was firm in the here and now, and instead of philosophizing about death, I looked at the empty armchair that had obviously been the one used by the deceased and symbolized now the person's presence with its touch of emptiness in a crowded room, and reflected on how I feel when a person I lived with and cared for dies and leaves forever what had been a long company. Before I can ask myself any question, there is a feeling that already tells me what I am going to find. If I feel bad, I know the reason. There are things I wanted to do for that person, things I wanted to tell him, but neglected to. I meant to reach out to her and let her know directly from me in an explicit expression my respect, appreciation, and affection. But days passed and occasions were missed and distance increased and the climate for intimacy became more rarified, and words became harder and were never spoken and now that person is dead. The person's ears can hear no longer what I wanted to say, things that would have given that person happiness and me peace on this day.

Death teaches me not to be too late in showing affection, not to delay expressing appreciation, not to postpone the kind deed, not to put off the brotherly word. Let me not reach the person's last day with the word unsaid and the good deed unaccomplished. Death is the great judge, not for the dead person, but for us who remain. How did I behave toward that person? I have no chance anymore to make things right before that person, and I have only my past behavior to go by. Was it satisfactory? If there was friction, was there also subsequent understanding? If there were distances, were there also prompt reconciliations? And above all, if there was silence, was there also communication, contact, expression? We often take for granted feelings and attitudes, assume that the other person knows perfectly well how we feel toward him or her, and a thin veil of shyness and laziness comes between us and prevents the explicit statement which is so very valuable if we can only have eyes to see it at the right moment.

Now the person is gone. Did the person know my true feelings toward him? Did I ever tell him? Did he guess? Did he doubt? I trust the person knew, but the fact is, I never told him clearly, directly, definitely. I really do not know what was in that person's mind toward me. And now I shall never know. That person is gone the silent way, and I am left with the nagging doubt of how I stood with that person, or rather, whether that person really knew how highly and appreciatively he or she stood with me. It would be a pity if I held him so highly and he never knew it.

It is said of Thomas Carlyle that he hid an affectionate nature behind a rough and blunt outward appearance. In particular, he had great and sincere love for his wife, but he did not usually show it, did not express it to her in loving words or tender behavior. He just took it for granted that she knew, and consequently did not take any trouble to speak about it and communicate his feelings directly. And so the years passed. His wife died before him, and then suddenly all the repressed affection in his heart surfaced violently and asked for an answer, for a certainty that his wife had known his love and treasured it. How could she answer now? He knew that his wife had kept a private diary through the years, and he searched for it, hoping to find in its pages the proof he belatedly needed. He found the diary and turned its pages in anxious haste. Nowhere could he find mention of his love for her, nowhere was there an allusion, a note, a reflection that would show she knew his love for her and valued it. On the contrary, on page after page he found distressing evidence of how his wife resented his temper and suffered under his frequent fits of anger. He searched through the mournful diary and could not find a single page where his love was reflected and accepted. And the great pity was that he did love his wife deeply; but he had never shown it to her. He then cried in useless despair: If she could come back to me now only for five minutes, only to let me tell her once how much I have loved her, how much she meant to me, how truly she was the center of my life and the joy of my heart; only five minutes to make sure that she knows now my feelings toward her, and then she can go, leaving me in peace once my heart is unburdened; but now it is too late and she will never come and I will carry to the day of my death the regret of not having told her in her life how much I loved her.

I said those things slowly, in an even voice, looking at the floor, as meditating with myself and by no means trying to make a speech or deliver a sermon to a formal audience. I paused for a while after saying those things, to see whether I wanted to continue or just stop there and say no more. I looked up and slowly focused on the faces around me. I noticed a woman of middle age and noble features. She was sitting motionless, and tears were gently flowing from her eyes. She was dressed in a plain white sari, and her forehead was bare: the red round turmeric mark between the eyes had been wiped clean. That meant she was a widow. Perhaps the widow of the man who had just died and in whose house I had spoken. In any case, her serene sorrow reflected better than my words the thought that was in my mind, and for a short while on my lips, of death as reminder of love.

Idle regret leads us nowhere. Fear of our own death is no gain to us. It is the certainty of our death and the repeated reminders of the deaths of others around us that can be beneficent and helpful in thoughtful contemplation. The one thing that gives satisfaction in the midst of a random existence is to do good to others and to know they have received our gift, to serve and to know that the service has reached, to say from the heart, "I love you," and to hear in answer from a fellow heart, "I know that you love me." That much we can do to light our path and enliven our fleeting existence. The danger is that years pass, occasions are missed, a kind of affective laziness, of genteel shame, comes over us and we hide the feelings and postpone the revelation. Later on. At the right moment. When a good chance comes. It never does. Life is short, for us and for others, and we can get the news of a person's death before we ever carry out our firm and definite resolution to tell him one day all the good things we felt in our heart for him. Now he will never know, and we are left with the gnawing regret of not having acted earlier, and waking up only when it is too late. Every death brings this message. One person is gone, but others remain; let us not then miss with others what we may have missed with this one. This turns sorrow into hope, despair into action, and shyness into love.

We are going to watch many deaths before our own during our lifetime. Welcome messengers of the necessary reminder. I look now at every person I love, I esteem, I work with, I pray for, and I tell myself: Before he goes, I want him to know what in my best mind I think of him, what I owe to him, what he has done for me. And before I myself go, I want them all to know how they stood with me in the true feelings of my sincere heart and my open love. If I revise the essential lesson at every death, this will be the best preparation for the day when my own death comes and I shall not be able to do anything anymore for anybody, and less to let them know. A day of death becomes, with this attitude, a day of learning.

I said no more. We remained still together for a good while in silence. I let myself sense the right moment to leave. I then stood up, walked slowly through the gathering with folded hands, and left. I hoped there were no more tears.

THE POWER OF FEARLESSNESS

In India the virtue of fearlessness has always been considered the basis of a good moral character. Only a fearless person can stand in the midst of the world and follow his principles against the constant pressure to do otherwise. It takes courage to tell the truth when a lie could make things easy and fast fill the pockets. It takes courage to be honest when people and circumstances press instantly toward dishonesty. It takes courage to reject invitations and stand criticism. It is only a truly fearless person who can find in himself or herself the courage to be true to himself no matter what others may think or say about him. Only a person without fear can be truly himself.

This is also the most precious blessing a man of God can bestow on a disciple. It is expressed by the right hand held vertically with its fingers straight and together, and its open palm facing the recipient of the blessing. The gesture means "the gift of fearlessness," and is wish and grace to infuse in the soul of the disciple the peace and courage that will enable him to face the world with joy and confidence. The palm is flat, meaning simplicity; the fingers are straight, meaning detachment, and they point to heaven from where strength comes to overcome fear.

The gesture and the Sanskrit expression that goes with it (abhay-dan) are used by common people in common life.

I have seen a boy appearing in fear before his father under the burden of a misbehavior that he is afraid will fetch him a punishment from his father, and before he could speak, I have seen the father, who knew the situation and the best way of dealing with it, raise his right hand slowly with open fingers pointed upward and pronounce in a low and almost unnecessary voice the well-known and welcome blessing. You have nothing to fear. Nothing from me in this case. I grant you the gift of fearlessness in your dealings with me. Tell me whatever you have to tell me, confess whatever you want to confess, and we will deal with the matter as person to person without any threats, fears, or punishments. You have nothing to fear.

Beautiful image and practice of the noblest virtue on earth. The blessing has a double edge to ensure the reign of fearlessness on all and from all. I do not want to be afraid of anybody, and I do not want anybody to be afraid of me. I grant from my part the gift of fearlessness to all who might have a reason to be afraid of me, and I claim for myself the same gift from anybody and anything that could possibly frighten me. My right hand raised in peaceful salutation to give and to receive the kindly waves of confidence and strength from all human beings and from all corners of the universe in a cosmic ritual of lasting peace.

Mahatma Gandhi knew these traditions and worked on them to prepare his people for the responsibility of independence. It was no small task to train a nation of hundreds of millions, who for centuries had lived under foreign rule, to take up the honor and the burden of ruling themselves with old convictions and new efficiency. And the first quality the Father of the Nation wanted in his people was fearlessness. That was the key to obtaining independence, and the key to governing the country once independence had been achieved. He planned his campaign of civil disobedience through a nonviolent struggle, and his only weapon in that singular battle was fearlessness. Do to us what you want; we will suffer it and come back in the same numbers to face you again with our peace and our rights. Put us in jail, harass us, kill us; we will not offer any resistance because we are not afraid of any consequences. We will not defend ourselves because there is nothing to defend. We are not afraid of death, and therefore we are not afraid of you. If a whole nation takes up such a stand, there is nothing it cannot achieve. The ultimate weapon an enemy can use is fear, and where there is no response to fear, his weapon is blunted.

Gandhi taught that nonviolence was not a weapon for cowards. The coward flies from danger or submits to unjust demands for fear of the harm that may come to him if he does not submit. That is not nonviolence but cowardice. The truly nonviolent persons do not fly from danger nor submit to unjust demands, but stand their ground with firm determination to suffer whatever may befall them in the respectful and peaceful defense of their rights. It takes more courage to resist defenseless than to fight blow for blow. Fearlessness is the basis of moral courage, and moral courage wins the true battles of history and of the soul.

Let me give an illustration of the way fearlessness was understood and practiced even by ordinary people in the struggle for independence, and of the results it obtained at the end. The event was the national protest Gandhi had organized against the salt laws. It was forbidden to the people to obtain salt from the sea, easy though it was, given the long coastline of India and the ready heat to evaporate seawater and leave the precious white relic. Salt was essential for the body under the constant perspiration of a tropical climate, was the elementary condiment to season the simplest food, and was also, in tradition and symbol, contract of fidelity and loyalty between any person and another "whose salt he had eaten." The salt, then, in its practical and emotional value, became the issue in the fight for independence while Gandhi exhorted the people to manufacture their own salt, and the government insisted in sending to jail those who did so, beginning with Gandhi himself.

It was in this context that the peaceful march into the government saltworks in Dharasana was organized. Groups of volunteers marched quietly in protest toward the gates of the factory and were detained there by soldiers who were well trained in wielding heavy clubs with an iron end that could break a skull at a single stroke. The volunteers, dressed in white, advanced slowly, about ten abreast, singing patriotic hymns, smiling into danger, steady in their step, while nurses waited on the side, ready to attend to the injuries that would inevitably occur. An American correspondent who witnessed the scene described with detailed horror what he saw. Line after line advanced, faced the police, were struck over the head by the heavy clubs, and were carried by the nurses to the hospital tents they had set up nearby. In one of the lines, the reporter described, was a Sikh volunteer, tall and hefty, who offered a striking contrast between his obvious physical strength and the defenseless innocence with which he was walking into the carnage. Facing him from the police line was a British sergeant who, on seeing him, braced himself for the encounter. When the volunteer approached within reach, the sergeant hit him with his club over the head with such a heavy blow that the victim dropped unconscious on the spot, his white turban lined with sudden red. The attending nurses withdrew him promptly and tended his wound. He soon came to, tested his strength, stood up, walked to the group, and took his place again in the next line to advance. There he was again facing the same sergeant in the same spot. When the sergeant saw him, he drew himself to full height, lifted his club, and got ready to strike his victim with doubled strength. The volunteer advanced slowly, in line with his companions, while the people around held their breath and watched in helpless horror the impending brutality.

The sergeant tensed himself and looked intently at the approaching man. He was now only a few steps away when something woke up inside the hardened reflexes of the army sergeant; the man in him recognized the true meaning of the situation against all the training and orders and routine that had ruled his life. He saw a wounded, defenseless man approach him with steady, dogged step; he saw his hurting smile and his firm determination; he remembered the time he had hit common thieves and base criminals and had almost enjoyed enforcing the law he represented against wrongdoers who harmed society. But this was a different man altogether; he was coming in peace and self-sacrifice for a noble cause with incredible courage. The soldier could fight anybody who would face him with any weapon in manly combat. But how could he hit a harmless victim in senseless cold blood? How could he lift his hand against a man who folded his in greeting? How could he use his weapon against one who had none?

The man had come now within striking distance of the raised club. At that moment the sergeant brought down his right arm slowly, placed his club under his left arm, brought his hand to his forehead in military salute to the brave volunteer, clicked his heels, turned around, and left the grounds. Fearlessness had won a heart. Not much later it would take a whole nation to freedom.

Powerful image and historic reality of what fearlessness is and can do in a person's life and in a country's history! True fearlessness is ultimately invincible. Hit me, strike me, wound me, kill me. What more can you do? And after doing all that, you realize that you have done nothing, that my cause is alive now more than ever, that you have only succeeded in showing your helplessness, that truth was on my side as courage was on my side, that your power is your weakness, and your victory is your defeat. If you strike a volunteer, there are thousands ready to take his place. The wave will go on and on until your arm gets tired and your club breaks. You will have to retreat, defeated by your own war machine. If you see that in time, you will withdraw honorably before the slaughter, and you will recognize in your heart that your might is powerless against a man who has no fear.

This attitude seems to be general in the Orient. A Japanese treatise on swordsmanship from the seventeenth century, quoted by D. T. Suzuki in *Zen and Japanese Culture*, tells the story of a Samurai who approached a master swordsman to be instructed in the art. The master first watched him do some fencing, and was impressed by his proficiency. He asked him who his previous master had been, in order to understand better what training he had received before. The Samurai stated that he had attended no school and followed no master, but had learned on his own by mere practice. The master said, "I know my job, and I can tell who is an ignorant and who is a master in my art. You are no ordinary swordsman, and your skill is of the first kind. You state however that you have not studied under any master, and if you say it it must be true, for a Samurai never lies. But think and tell me whether there is a secret in your life, an experience or an attitude that makes you be so advanced in an art which others take so long to learn." The Samurai thought and answered, "There is one thing in my life which marks all my actions and rules all my thoughts. When I was a boy it was impressed upon me that a Samurai must not be afraid of death, and I have grappled for years with that thought and that ideal till now I am totally free from the fear of death. Maybe this is the explanation you required." The master replied, "You have said it. The ultimate secret of swordsmanship is fearlessness in the face of death. He who masters this, masters the art. You are free from the fear of death, and you have nothing more to learn."[*]

Fear of death inhibits reflexes, blocks reactions, and blinds the eye. Under such circumstances the combat is lost before it has begun. No training and no learning will do any good if the faculties of mind and body are bound by the instinctive fear of death. But once this fear is conquered, the mind is free and the body relaxed, each move is anticipated and each thrust is parried, and the free swordsman dances his way into easy victory.

Martial arts in the Japanese tradition are mirror and school for life. And this supreme lesson holds good for the art of living as it does for fencing or wrestling or archery or judo or karate. Banish all fears from your heart before you enter the contest. Do not be afraid of death if you want to enjoy life. Take death for granted, accept it, welcome it, and then be free to obtain the best of each moment, all the more valuable because it can be the last. Fearlessness releases our best faculties, the virgin eye, the guiltless joy, the spontaneous wonder. The degree to which we are free from fears will mark the degree to which we are worthy of life.

[*] D. T. Suzuki, *Zen and Japanese Culture* (Princeton, N.J.: Princeton University Press, 1959).

LOOK AT YOUR FEAR

Jiddu Krishnamurti had this to say on fear:

At the actual moment as I am sitting here I am not afraid; I am not afraid in the present, nothing is happening to me, nobody is threatening me or taking anything away from me. But beyond the actual moment there is a deeper layer in the mind which is consciously or unconsciously thinking of what might happen in the future or worrying that something from the past may overtake me. So I am afraid of the past and of the future. I have divided time into the past and the future. Thought steps in, says, "Be careful it does not happen again," or "Be prepared for the future. The future may be dangerous for you. You have got something now but you may lose it. You may die tomorrow, your wife may run away, you may lose your job. You may never become famous. You may be lonely. You want to be quite sure of tomorrow." . . . Therefore thought is responsible for fear. This is so, you can see it for yourself. When you are confronted with something immediately there is no fear. It is only when thought comes in that there is fear. Therefore our question now is, is it possible for the mind to live completely, totally, in the present? It is only such a mind that has no fear.*

* Jiddu Krishnamurti, *Freedom from the Known* (London: Victor Gollancz, Ltd., 1977), 46.

The words are tantalizingly true; they are a pressing invitation to that simplest and loftiest of all states of the soul: living the present. Fear is a creature of shadows, of memory or projection, of regret or anticipation. As soon as the fear is brought under the light of the present, it dissolves into the nothingness it came from. It is thought that brings fear. If we still the thought, the fear will vanish.

I look around and there is nothing threatening me at the moment. Nobody is pointing a loaded gun at me, the ceiling of my room is as solid as it could be and shows no signs of collapsing and falling on me, I do not feel hungry or cold or sick, and even the telephone, my only vulnerable opening to the outside world, is at this moment mercifully quiet. So far as I am here, I am fine, and no impending calamity threatens me in any way. If I were able to be where I am and to do what I do, I would be fine and I would not know what fear is.

But then thought comes in. Between paragraph and paragraph of this page I am writing, or rather, more exactly and shamefully and disturbingly, at the middle of a sentence, left unfinished with glaring irresponsibility, that irrepressible thought of mine starts jumping about and creating spaces of uneasiness in my mind. In a few days I have to travel, and the reservation is not confirmed. Shall I cancel? Shall I take the risk? Shall I inform my hosts of the possible hitch so that they postpone the engagements they had planned for me? Shall I . . . ? But what was I writing? I look at the unfinished sentence with shame and remorse. No idea how I had meant to complete it. I can scratch it and begin anew, or finish it somehow, hoping the patch will not show. Let me get down to it. But before I settle to the work, my jumpy imagination starts its game again. Now it makes me worry. If this is the way I write books, nobody is going to read them. If I cannot concentrate enough to finish even a sentence, and leave off at the middle without previous notice and then I no longer remember how I had meant to finish it and start all over again and lose track again and (as is happening to me at this very moment) I do not remember how I began this sentence and have no idea how I can finish it with dignity . . . Where was I? My unruly imagination has taken me away from the present, and has brought worry, uncertainty, and fear. If only I could stick my nose to my typewriter, my mind would be all this while free from fears.

This is a clear behavioral equation: Mind in the present is mind without fears, and mind in past and future is breeding ground for all kinds of fears. Reality is fearlessness, and imagination is trepidation. Contact with facts brings equanimity, objectivity, freshness, whereas flights into fancy land us eventually in insecurity and apprehension. Our thought never stops, and so when we stop feeding it with present material, it jumps immediately into past or future and ruins our peace. Theoretically there are two ways of preventing thought from bolting away in space: One is to keep it on the task in hand, and another to stop it altogether. This second option is hard in practice and likely impossible in theory, though Krishnamurti himself claimed he could walk alone for hours without a thought crossing his mind: rare achievement of a lofty soul. For most of us the practical way to tame the mind and preclude fears will be to focus thought on the present reality, to befriend our senses, to open our eyes, to enlarge our lungs and activate our skin, to take in moment by moment with sensorial innocence all the impressions that reach our bodily outposts and use them as welcome mooring to anchor our attention on the shore of reality.

Our senses live essentially in the present, and to discover them is to enter into the joyful adventure of light and sound that is life at each instant on this solid earth under the open sky. Fear is in the mind, not in the senses, and a return to the senses is the way to lasting fearlessness.

Still, thought will remain, and with it fear. What to do then? Krishnamurti advises: Just look at it. When fear lifts its head above the horizon of conscious thought, just look at it. Take a good look; do not avoid it, do not run away from it, do not try to rationalize or neutralize or exorcize it; do not call it bad, do not judge, do not reject; just let it be. If you become the judge who wants to condemn fear, you are unwittingly inviting it. By pushing it away, you bring it closer, as also by trying to ignore it forcibly, you make it more real. Do not resist it, but simply look at it in the face, observe it, watch it. This neutral observation can by itself reduce considerably the effect of fear on our nerves, or even suppress it altogether. This, Krishnamurti says, is "learning to live with fear." His words:

> Can you watch fear without any conclusion, without any interference of the knowledge you have accumulated about it? If you cannot, then what you are watching is the past, not fear; if you can, then you are watching fear for the first time without the interference of the past. You can watch only when the mind is very quiet, just as you can listen to what someone is saying only when your mind is not chattering with itself, carrying on a dialogue with itself about its own problems and anxieties. Can you in the same way look at your fear without trying to resolve it, without bringing in its opposite, courage— actually look at it and not try to escape from it? When you say, "I must control it, I must get rid of it, I must understand it," you are trying to escape from it. You

can observe a cloud or a tree or the movement of a river with a fairly quiet mind because they are not very important to you, but to watch yourself is far more difficult because there the demands are so practical, the reactions so quick. So when you are directly in contact with fear or despair, loneliness or jealousy, or any other ugly state of mind, can you look at it so completely that your mind is quiet enough to see it?*

I feel afraid. The alarm of fear has sounded in the recesses of my mind. The red light is on. A concrete fear of an impending danger, big or small, but enough to upset me, tenses my nerves and quickens my heartbeat. Or it may be an abstract, general fear, a sense of foreboding, a disgust with things as they are and an ominous conviction that they are going to get worse. The ghost of fear, in any of its varied manifestations, has loomed on my consciousness, and I feel unsettled. I can try to distract myself. It works for a while. I get immersed in work, seek a colleague to discuss business with, go for a walk, or enter into prayer. All is fine. But while I am engaged in these worthy activities, the dark memory of the threatening fear stalks my every step from the twilight of my consciousness. There it is. I cannot forget it. After dodging it for a while, it pops up again, every time with an uglier rictus on its face, at a closer distance from my heart. The more I try to forget it, the more I remember it. Yes, I am afraid. And I know it is bad to be afraid, so I judge myself, I condemn myself, I pity myself, I put myself down. I am ashamed to be afraid. I create a whole screen of black feelings around my helpless mind. The fear will come up again and again

* Jiddu Krishnamurti, *Freedom from the Known* (London: Victor Gallancz, Ltd., 1977), 46.

with greater strength each time; and when at long last it goes by, being contradicted by facts or by the sheer weariness of waiting, it will leave me weakened and defeated, and afraid once more of the next fear, which will not take long in appearing now. That way lies only misery and despair.

Let me change my stand. Fear has come up. I see it. I feel afraid of something that is going to mean trouble to me, even serious trouble. And the fear of it is there facing me and challenging me. Let it be. I look at it with inward detachment. I do not analyze, I do not complain, I do not try to understand why this has happened and why now and why to me. Much less do I try to resolve the situation and banish the fear. I just look in peace. Yes, I am afraid . . . and it is fine. I feel worried at the impending danger, and, well, yes, I am worried and I know it and there is no more to it. I do not cry for help or do not rally for action. I do not react one way or another. I do not even go out of my way in the other direction and try to accept the situation, just as I do not try to reject it. I let it be. I watch. I wait. I stay with the fear. I live with it. No anxiety about when it will go or what it will do. Not for me to settle that. I am just an impartial observer of a neutral happening. I am watching myself, watching my mind, watching my fear. I let things happen. I watch the show.

Once in Trevor Tal, of which I have spoken, I met a wild bear. I had heard a low grunt in the underwood, and curiously, foolishly, recklessly, I went closer to investigate. The bear was on all fours, but turned to me and stood on its hind legs for a moment to welcome me. It was black, with a large white V across its breast, as must have been the fashion among its kind that season. Nice pattern for a sweater. I looked at him. I could distinguish each nail in his paws, long and thick, a self-grown armory of deadly scimitars. I noticed the varied shades of his long hair, the black wet muzzle, the naked teeth. He came down on all fours and looked at me with the same calm and interest with which I was looking at him. There was in me no desire to run away, no desire to go after him, no move to flee, and no intent to prolong the interview; just the quiet contemplation of that fine specimen of nature for as long as he would be pleased to offer himself to my sight. The bear, on his part, did not seem inclined to deepen his acquaintance with me either, and after he gave me the once-over, he turned his rump unceremoniously toward me and trotted away down the valley to his lair. Only when he was gone did I realize how foolish I had been to court danger in the unequal meeting. My manicured nails would not have gone far against his hairy paws if it had come to a handshake. Though maybe there was not so much danger after all. There had been just passive observation, no provocation, no contempt. I had not even signaled the bear in any established language to go away and leave me alone. That is why he eventually did it. He understood because I had not spoken.

I had looked a bear in the face. Can I look my own fears in the face? Maybe that is the only way to make them go.

DO NOT FEAR!

When the angels announced the coming of Jesus to the shepherds of Bethlehem, their first words were, "Do not fear"; and when they brought to the women in Jerusalem the news of the Resurrection of Jesus, they began again, "Do not fear." It would seem that the message that Jesus comes to bring to men and women with his presence on earth and his death on the cross is the abolishing of fear from our hearts. And it would also seem that the message goes largely unheeded, as the angels had to repeat at the end what they had said at the beginning. The last lesson in the angelic manual for humanity's redemption is the same as the first: "Do not fear."

"Why are you afraid, men of little faith?" "Rise and have no fear." "Fear not, daughter of Zion." To Zachary, to Mary, to Peter, to the disciples, to the crowds, comes the cheering message, the good news that will change the course of history and the face of the world. Do not fear. This is a new age. We are free. We are no more under bondage and are not to fear the forces of nature, the powers of darkness, the scruples of our own soul.

When man broke his first innocence in Paradise, his immediate reaction was fear. "I heard the sound as you were walking in the garden, and I was afraid." And afraid he continued to be through desert and cities, by day and by night, in his heart and in his society, wherever he lived and whatever he did. Afraid of God's steps, afraid of his own step; afraid of strangers and afraid of friends; afraid for his body and afraid for his soul; afraid to live and afraid to die. A long chain of fears from first breath to last in a land of shadows. Because man had lost his innocence, he was condemned to live subject to fear.

And fear spoiled his joy. A sword of Damocles hung on every pleasure, and its menace ruined the enjoyment. Live, but you shall die; eat, but you may get poisoned; travel, but you may meet with an accident; love, but you may be hurt. Every human activity had its dark shadow attached to it, and food got mixed with ashes in the mouth. The possession of a treasure is forever linked with the fear of losing it; and the detachment of living without treasures brings the greater fear of how long the detachment will last in a world of allurements. Nothing is sure, nothing is safe; and life without safety is life with trepidation.

Insecurity works on our nerves. We become tense and project our inner tensions on the world around. We see others as enemies, and opportunities as threats. Work is competition and life a battlefield. We fear the dangers we know, and even more, the dangers we don't know but suspect at every corner we turn. A fear that can be named loses its terror and blunts its edge, but a fear without a name, a ghost without a face, dark as a shadow and swift as a storm, increases its fright and paralyzes action. Nameless fear that haunts relentlessly the secret weakness of mortal man.

Redemption is liberation from fear. Look up, fill your breast, lift your head, open your smile, and welcome life. The strength of fearlessness and the joy of courage. This is the meaning of redemption. The faculty to stand in confidence before God, and in consequence, before all people and the whole of creation to work in freedom and live with joy. This is the work of Jesus on earth. Do not fear, he is born. Do not fear, he is risen. God is literally on our side, and if God is with us, who is against us? We know now that every person is sacred, and every situation is grace. "All things work out for the best in favor of those who love God." His hand is behind every event, his face in every cloud. Things make sense because he knows, and life is joy because it leads to him. No more fear in a world Jesus has walked, in the hearts he visits daily. The old curse holds no more where eyes are opened to the supreme reality of the world as God's creation and life as his gift.

This is faith. The new perspective. The view from the mountain. The clear sky. The straight road. From the new vantage point there are no ambushes, no dark corners, no fears. "And God saw that it was good." With him we too see it now. Life is good. Nature is kind. Suffering has a meaning, and death leads to life. We do not ignore suffering, try to hide it, or avoid it when it is unavoidable, but we seek to conquer in Christ the permanent, irrational, craven fear of future, imaginary, shadowy sufferings that make us miserable before they come and make us experience many false, imaginary trials before the only real one comes. We will face suffering when it comes, as it will definitely come in the trial this life is, but we refuse to be cowed by its thought, harassed by its anticipation, wounded by its fear.

We take things as they come and face life as it is. When a dark cloud appears on the horizon, we do mark it, but we do not miss the calm of the present sunshine because of the storm we fear will come later. The storm may blow over before it reaches us; but if it discharges over our heads, we know how to find shelter in time, or, ultimately, we are ready to get wet and repair the damage it may cause. But we do not lose heart. We find the courage that defeats fear in the faith we have in Jesus, who has walked our way before us and now stands at our side to lead us on to victory with him. "No affliction, hardship, persecution, hunger, nakedness, peril or death can separate us from the love of Christ," said Saint Paul. And John offered the golden link: "Perfect love casts out fear." Our faith in Jesus seals our love, which eliminates fear from our lives.

This is Jesus' own final word to us: "Do not be afraid. I have overcome the world."